COURTYARDS FOR
MODERN LIVING

ACKNOWLEDGMENTS

I would like to thank all the designers and owners featured in this book. Their dedication in commissioning these wonderful outdoor spaces is clearly expressed in the pages that follow.

Thanks must also go to the many photographers who contributed to this project. I would also like to thank my partner Naomi for her support and literary criticism.

Stephen Crafti

COURTYARDS FOR MODERN LIVING

Stephen Crafti

Contemporary Outdoor Spaces

images
Publishing

Published in Australia in 2008 by

The Images Publishing Group Pty Ltd

ABN 89 059 734 431

6 Bastow Place, Mulgrave, Victoria 3170, Australia

Tel: +61 3 9561 5544 Fax: +61 3 9561 4860

books@imagespublishing.com

www.imagespublishing.com

National Library of Australia Cataloguing-in-Publication entry

Author:	Crafti, Stephen, 1959–
Title:	Courtyards for modern living : contemporary outdoor spaces / Stephen Crafti.
ISBN:	978 1 86470 282 8 (hbk.)
Subjects:	Outdoor living spaces.
	Gardens—design.
	Landscape architecture.
Dewey Number:	728.93

Edited by Beth Browne

Designed by The Graphic Image Studio Pty Ltd, Mulgrave, Australia
www.tgis.com.au

Pre-publishing services by Splitting Image Colour Studio Pty Ltd, Australia
Printed by Everbest Printing Co. Ltd., in Hong Kong/China

IMAGES has included on its website a page for special notices in relation to this
and our other publications. Please visit www.imagespublishing.com.

CONTENTS

INTRODUCTION

Gardens have changed significantly over the last couple of decades. In the 1980s for example, it wasn't uncommon to have manicured lawns framed with box hedges and annuals. With their owners ignoring how much water these gardens required for maintenance, these European-style gardens multiplied across Australia, both in city and rural environments.

This fussy European style of gardening could have continued unabated had there not been severe water restrictions across Australia in the past few years. With pruned garden beds faltering under such dry conditions, there's been a gradual progression to more low-maintenance gardens, often featuring hardy drought-tolerant indigenous species. Native grasses have been replacing water-thirsty flowers, with colour often seen in leaves rather than petals. Along with the changed conditions has come the rediscovery of succulent plants, popular in the 1950s.

Another significant change in garden design has been the result of a move to larger houses on smaller sites. In many cases, the backyard has been reduced to a strip of turf. And the available outdoor space often takes the form of a courtyard accessed from kitchen and living areas. Paved, rather than planted, these courtyards are treated as an outdoor room, rather than a garden in the traditional sense. Filled with a few potted plants, an outdoor dining setting and often a built-in barbeque, these courtyards are used for alfresco dining. Given Australia's climate, these 'rooms' can be used for a considerable part of the year.

Stephen Crafti

The size of the outdoor space has decreased in relation to the size of homes being built, together with a reduction in land holdings. With increased property prices, having a large garden that's rarely used is considered decadent. Even those with the means to maintain a large garden often prefer spending time on other activities such as travel and entertainment.

With the outdoor room forming a new style of garden, there has been a move to look at the house and garden in a more holistic way. There's an attempt to link the house with the garden or courtyard. Floor finishes are carried through from the inside to the outside. And in many cases, large sliding or folding glass doors allow the two spaces to blend together.

In the past, architects operated independently from landscape architects or landscape designers. Once the new house or extension was completed, the landscape would go in as an afterthought, often disconnected from the architecture. However, the indoors and outdoors are increasingly being treated as one.

In other instances, the connection to the outdoors is more structural. The kitchen bench may extend beyond glass doors to the courtyard-style garden. Complete with barbeque and sink, meals can be prepared outside.

Some architects align courtyard walls to interior walls to create a seamless transition between the interior and exterior. Generous eaves not only form part of the architecture, but also allow outdoor spaces to be protected from the harsher sunlight. In some instances the courtyards have full sun, with market umbrellas creating shade where needed. Pergolas have also become popular. Trained with creepers, they allow filtered light into the interior spaces.

One of the major issues raised in this book is sustainability. Increasingly, people are requesting low-maintenance gardens that require little attention, both in terms of water consumption and in the physical care of plants. Many labour-intensive plants have been replaced with drought-resistant native plants. Another feature of many gardens are rainwater tanks, used to collect rainwater used for garden beds and lawns. And while some tanks are concealed below timber decks, others are prominently featured in the garden.

Stone feature walls and ponds are becoming more prevalent, along with outdoor sculptures, chairs and tables, some freestanding, others built-in. One courtyard garden featured in this book includes only a few plants, mainly creepers along a fence to create privacy from neighbours. The main feature in the courtyard is banquette-style seating, extending from the meals area inside the kitchen/living area almost to the back fence. Where possible, sustainable materials are used, from recycled timber awnings to furniture, and plantation timbers are favoured over endangered species.

Some of the most innovative gardens in this book contain not much more than a single tree. One garden, for example, features bluestone paving on one side of the garden, and a pond on the other. Designed to appear shattered, the pond features granite forms, loosely arranged. The only tree is a Japanese maple, elevated in a bluestone bed. Another courtyard garden features a single Chinese elm. The elm has been carefully placed to create filtered light into the main bedroom. The elm also allows seasonal changes to be observed, with its leaves turning to gold in autumn.

Some of the gardens featured in this book have a strong contemporary Japanese feel. Large rocks, strategically placed, are framed with bamboo and maples. Lawn is replaced by a pond or shallow pool of water, often accompanied by a water feature. These low-maintenance gardens not only require little attention, but also create a tranquil ambience for adjoining dining or living areas.

While the formal parterre-style garden may be disappearing, other trends in gardening are becoming stronger. Herb gardens near kitchens are becoming more popular and smaller courtyards are carefully positioned as extensions of living and bedroom areas. And unlike the formal gardens, there's a sense of spontaneity in the way gardens are planned. There's less excessive pruning and clipping, with trees and shrubs allowed to find their own forms.

The gardens featured in this book are varied. Some are densely planted, while others are minimal, with a single tree. These rich and varied gardens share a common theme: suitability for 21st-century living.

SKEW PYRAMID

Architects Mauro Baracco and Louise Wright see gardens as an extension of their architecture. 'We couldn't tell you where architecture stops and landscape begins', says Wright, who clearly demonstrates this approach in this 1970s house. One of a pair, the architect-designed home originally had a few scraggy native plants in the front garden. 'We love native gardens by Gordon Ford and Ellis Stones (respected designers from the 1960s and 1970s). But this wasn't one of them', she adds.

As the two clinker brick homes have a striking similarity, Baracco + Wright Architects treated the two front gardens as one. While the neighbouring house had undercover parking at the front, the owners of this house could only access the garage via a narrow concrete driveway along one side. 'Access was extremely tight', says Wright, who transformed the garage into a covered outdoor room for the owner's children.

The other problem with the front garden was its lack of privacy and the narrow front balcony leading from the living areas was too small for table and chairs. The solution was to create a skew pyramid-shaped 'mound' across the two properties, which reaches its peak outside the main living area. The front of the site was excavated by approximately 1.5 metres and a garage with a tilted steel roller door (inclined 45 degrees) was created. 'We exaggerated the natural geography of the site to create privacy for the house. Previously headlights would shine straight into our client's living room', says Wright, who extended the line of the fibro cement balustrade to create further privacy.

ARCHITECT
Baracco + Wright Architects

PLANT SELECTION
Essence Gardens

The front garden is slowly being covered with maidenhair creepers, as well as native grasses, dwarfed eucalypts, native broom, bottlebrush and grevillea. 'We wanted to maintain the abstract quality of the form. The maidenhair is quite fine and dense. Eventually, this creeper will spill over the balustrade', says Wright, who was assisted with plant selection by Izabella Meraviglia-Crivelli of Essence Gardens.

The original concrete driveway was removed. Maidenhair creeper cascades down the garage's side elevation and the concrete has been replaced with circular concrete pavers. 'The circles have a certain pop feel', says Wright, who knew the owners had an affinity for this sensibility.

The front terrace can no longer be seen from the street. And what was once a narrow balcony extending the width of the house is now a generous terrace with views of the city skyline in the distance. 'We wanted to engage with the street rather than turn our backs on it', says Baracco, who was surprised by the ease of obtaining a planning permit for the design from the local council. 'Normally the garage has to be hidden in the back garden. But they could see the merit of what we were trying to achieve', he adds.

PHOTOGRAPHY BY **Aaron Pocock**

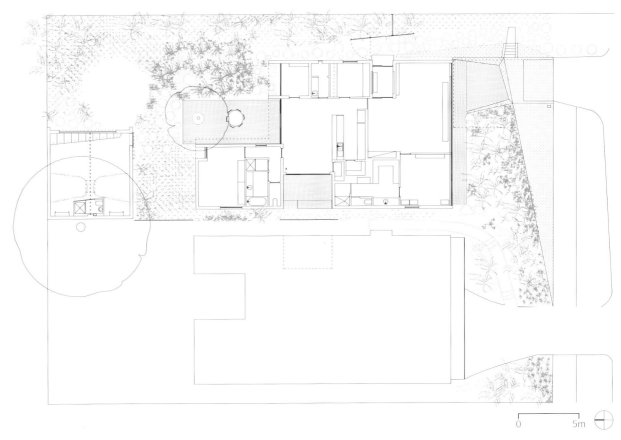

INSIDER'S TIP

Use plants that are
appropriate to the style of
house as well as appropriate
to the soil conditions.
Indigenous species will be
suitable for even the most
difficult soil.

0   5m

RESPONDING TO THE ARCHITECTURE

Landscape designer Jack Merlo was keen to respond to this two-storey house, designed by Wood Marsh Architects. Nestled behind a split-faced limestone tile wall, the rectilinear form required a unique garden.

Merlo responded to the architect's design by creating a pebbled front garden with loosely planted Mt. Fuji ornamental cherry trees. The five loosely arranged trees soften the façade, while adding texture to the garden. The trees feature a white double blossom in spring, with leaves turning to reds and oranges during autumn. 'I didn't want to make the garden appear too formal', says Merlo, who contrasted the linear bluestone path to the front door with more randomly placed stepping-stones in the garden bed.

'At night each tree is up-lit, so it appears more dramatic', he adds. And to create a feel of the garden flowing into the interior, the pebbles in the front bed extend beyond the feature wall and can be seen from the glass floor at the end of a living area.

While the front garden bed is quite minimal, the plantings around the periphery of the house are considerably denser. Evergreen plants, such as magnolias, ensure privacy from neighbours.

ARCHITECT
Wood Marsh Architects

LANDSCAPE DESIGNER
Jack Merlo Design

The rear garden originally featured a swimming pool. The old spa was removed and steps to the pool were realigned to create a rectilinear form, like the house. And to create a sharper edge to the pool, the corners were squared off to create a cleaner and more contemporary look. In addition to remodelling the pool, a glass and concrete pavilion was added as a cabana. Complete with gymnasium and bathroom facilities, there's no need to drag wet towels through the house. 'Privacy was a major issue in designing the back garden', says Merlo, referring to the apartments next door. To add depth to the side planting, a row of agave succulents was planted, together with ornamental grasses.

To alleviate the problem of overlooking, Merlo planted lilly-pilly trees on both side boundaries and trained them as an evergreen hedge. And to create a vista, as well as another layer, a second tier of ornamental capital pear trees were planted adjacent to the pool. 'The pear trees are quite upright and they tend to grow up rather than out', says Merlo. To reduce the amount of concrete surrounding the pool, grass squares appear at the base of each pear tree.

'The idea was a fairly low-maintenance garden. The owners didn't want to have to keep fishing leaves out of the pool. These pear trees only drop leaves for two to three weeks every year', says Merlo.

PHOTOGRAPHY BY **Peter Clarke, Latitude**

16

INSIDER'S TIP

The garden should complement the architecture. There should be a sense of connection, whether from the materials used or the way they're used.

REWORKING
A CLASSIC

Architect-designed in 1968, this house was blessed with great bones and generous spaces. Oriented towards a northern rear garden and located in a quiet cul de sac, the house was waiting for a new lease of life. 'The floor plan wasn't significantly altered. But the connection to the garden was improved', says designer Jack Merlo, who worked with Emma Tulloch of Nixon Tulloch Architecture.

Originally, there was a small fernery in the undercroft area at the front of the house. But plants were struggling to survive with restricted light opportunities. So the front garden was completely reworked, starting from the front nature strip, which Merlo redesigned with bluestone paving, surrounded by mondo grass. Two Chinese elms were planted in front of the house.

A new high brick fence was added to the front garden, creating an enclosed courtyard. The courtyard now features a shallow pond, together with two different levels of planting: jasmine, which provides ground cover on the lower level, and agave succulents and Hills evergreen fig planted at the higher level. 'I wanted to carry the bluestone paving in front through to the entrance', says Merlo. While the front garden is

ARCHITECT | LANDSCAPE DESIGNER
Nixon Tulloch Architecture | **Jack Merlo Design**

ornamental rather than a place to sit, Merlo ensured the architects provided vistas of the courtyard.

While the rear garden is oriented to enjoy maximum sunlight, it was originally eight to nine steps below the home's floor level. With a narrow balcony that ran the width of the living area, there was little connection to the garden. Merlo raised the back garden to a level that is only a few steps down from the new terrace. And to create a more dynamic arrangement, the 3-by-9-metre swimming pool was 'cut' into the rear terrace. Water now laps at the edge of the living room. Complete with a wet edge, the swimming pool provides an important vista from the house.

Merlo also added depth to the back garden by planting succulents in a raised bed together with ornamental pear trees. Evergreen figs were planted on the back boundary and fronted by a row of small white hydrangeas for softness and colour. To link the front and back gardens, timber features on the new garage door and the side fences. 'Before the garden and house were treated independently. The terrace now works as another room', says Merlo, who requested the architects extend the nib walls and canopy for sun protection.

PHOTOGRAPHY BY **Shannon McGrath**

INSIDER'S TIP

A back garden should be used as well as being integral to the house. If the connection to the house isn't there, it will simply remain unused.

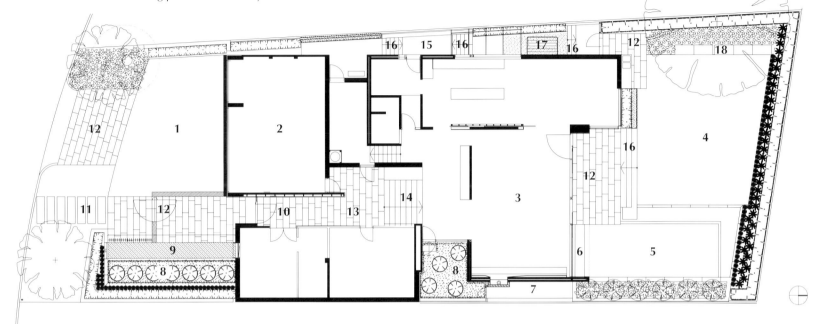

1 Driveway
2 Garage
3 Residence
4 Lawn
5 Swimming pool
6 Swim-out ledge
7 Pool equipment area
8 Massed groundcover
9 Reflective pond
10 Entry
11 Bluestone stepping stones
12 Sawn bluestone paving
13 Honed bluestone paving
14 Timber steps
15 Concrete landing
16 Steps
17 Clothesline
18 Stone bench

TREES ONLY

This family home occupies a reasonably large site. However, although there was room for numerous garden beds, the owners requested only trees. 'Our clients wanted a leafy outlook, but they didn't want to have to spend every weekend in the garden', says architect Rob Mills, who worked closely with landscape designer Annie Wilkes of Parterre Garden, Sydney.

To maximise the natural sunlight on the property, Mills located the two-storey brick and rendered house towards the rear of the site. 'I also wanted to set up the sight lines through the house, so the vistas became more impressive', says Mills. While there is a small courtyard-style garden to the rear of the home, the largest portion of the garden is at the front. As there are glass windows and doors on either side of the open-plan living areas, the two garden areas appear as one continuous element in the design.

Mills located the front door towards the rear of the site. A walled path, lined with concrete pavers and framed with evergreen trees, creates the impression of space. 'We also wanted to create privacy from the pool', says Mills. The focal point of the front garden is the 15-metre swimming pool, designed to reach the edge of the living areas. Its simple lineal form is only broken up by two golden-brown urns at either end, which are used as water features.

ARCHITECT
Rob Mills

LANDSCAPE DESIGNER
Annie Wilkes, Parterre Garden

In keeping with the owner's brief for 'trees only', the front and rear garden are planted with Manchurian pear trees, partially bordering the pool and front fence. 'The pear trees offer privacy. They're a great species for screening', says Mills, who also appreciates their branch form and changing leaf colour during autumn. 'The design is really a series of rectangles sitting beside each other', says Mills.

And although the garden is minimally planted, it's one of the most used parts of the house. Complete with outdoor setting, the front terrace acts as another room, the perfect setting for alfresco dining.

PHOTOGRAPHY BY **Gerald Warrener; Andrew Ashton**

INSIDER'S TIP

Try and capture as much space as possible. You can create a sense of a space going on indefinitely if sight lines are planned correctly.

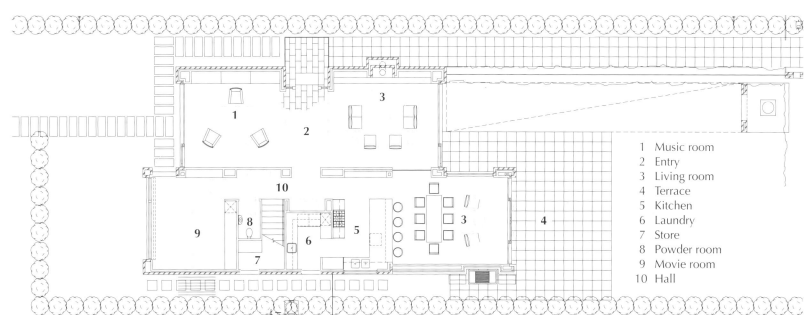

1 Music room
2 Entry
3 Living room
4 Terrace
5 Kitchen
6 Laundry
7 Store
8 Powder room
9 Movie room
10 Hall

ONE LEVEL

While this two-storey terrace had a relatively deep back garden, it was rarely used. Spread over a number of levels, the garden was overgrown and reasonably dark. 'We had to remove a couple of pine trees. The light wasn't getting into the house', says architect Tony Freeman, a director of Molnar Freeman Architects.

The other problem with the property was the lack of on-site car parking, with the owners having to park their cars on the street. The architects were fortunate on two counts; one being access to the rear of the property via a laneway, and the second being the significant slope of the land towards the rear. Molnar Freeman Architects designed a double garage at the rear and created an entirely new garden, all at one level, above this.

The terrace was completely reworked with double-height living spaces at the rear. Featuring floor-to-ceiling glass bi-fold doors and louvred highlight glass windows, there's now a strong connection to the garden. A new timber deck was added to the rear, designed around an established jacaranda tree. Complete with barbeque and outdoor setting, it's a useable back garden, as well as being aesthetically pleasing.

ARCHITECT   LANDSCAPE DESIGNER
Molnar Freeman Architects   **Anthony Wyer**

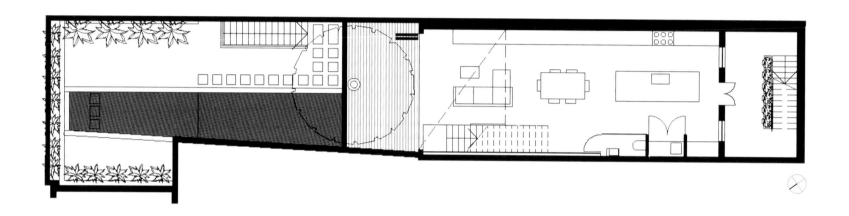

As the depth of the site is generous, the architects were able to include a 16-metre lap pool. Part of the lap pool extends over the garage, where it is only 300 millimetres deep. 'At that point, it's more of a reflective pond. But even that small extension creates a greater sense of depth in the garden', says Freeman, who included a small lawn adjacent to the pool.

Molnar Freeman worked with landscape designer Anthony Wyer in designing the garden. Rusted steel planter boxes were incorporated in the design and suitable low-maintenance shrubs were selected, including New Zealand Christmas bush, tiger grass, lay palm and slender mat rush.

Another issue was the need to create privacy from adjacent neighbours. As a result, timber batten screens were designed for the rear side boundaries that will eventually be covered with bougainvillea. 'Colour was part of our brief', says Freeman, who inserted LED lights in the pool. 'At night, you're drawn to the pool. And during the day, there's the dramatic purplish red of the bougainvillea', he adds.

PHOTOGRAPHY BY **Murray Fredericks**

INSIDER'S TIP

The garden should be treated as if it is part of the dwelling. With this house, you're drawn to the garden as soon as you walk past the front door.

LANDING IN A FIELD

This house, designed by McBride Charles Ryan (MCR), appears to have landed in a field. With its 'shattered' copper domed roof, some of the parts seem to have broken off. MCR's concept-driven design required a soft landing from landscape designers Eckersley Stafford Design 'The brief from MCR was to make the plants appear as though they were pushing through the house, like tufts of grass emerging from under a rock', says designer Rick Eckersley. 'The owner also wanted to see an array of greenery from all windows in the house', he adds.

The front garden is dominated by an established oak tree. There was never any question about its removal, and the tree was to be disturbed as little as possible during the construction period. As the dome meets the ground plain, there's a bed of soft planting that includes sacred bamboo, fine leafed carex, *Liriope* and aspidistra. 'We've used a variety of different grasses as well as different leaf types. The idea was to create a soft and wispy edge to the home's more jagged edges', says Eckersley, who mixed natives with exotic plants. As the garden beds develop, the exposed aggregate paths that wrap around the house will become less dominant.

ARCHITECT
McBride Charles Ryan

LANDSCAPE DESIGNER
Eckersley Stafford Design

The front courtyard-style garden also features a sitting area with a table and chairs as well as a couple of moveable timber benches. While part of the terrace area is protected with the domed roof, an adjacent area is open to the sky. One of the most significant plants in this courtyard is elephant ears, which, though it has an unspectacular flower, was selected for its great perfume. 'On a still summer night, the scent wafts through the entire house and garden', says Eckersley.

The design of the garden was partially informed by the colour scheme used by McBride Charles Ryan. Interior designer Debbie-Lyn Ryan gave Eckersley a montage of the finished colours. The brownish copper colour of the roof, for example, is picked up in the leaves of the sacred bamboo. Likewise, the green of the external tiles appears in many of the plants.

The rear garden features many of the grasses and shrubs used in the front garden. But while the focus is on the oak tree in the front garden, the rear garden features a jacaranda tree, planted within a timber deck. 'Eventually the jacaranda will cover the whole deck', says Eckersley, who planted mondo grasses under the tree and goddess lilies around it.

As the house is located on a fairly compact site, Eckersley was keen to disguise the perimeter as much as possible, borrowing views from a neighbouring garden (also designed by Eckersley). 'I wanted the garden to feel generous, as though it went on forever. But I also wanted to ensure that you could enjoy the garden from every aspect within the house', he adds.

PHOTOGRAPHY BY **Rick Eckersley**

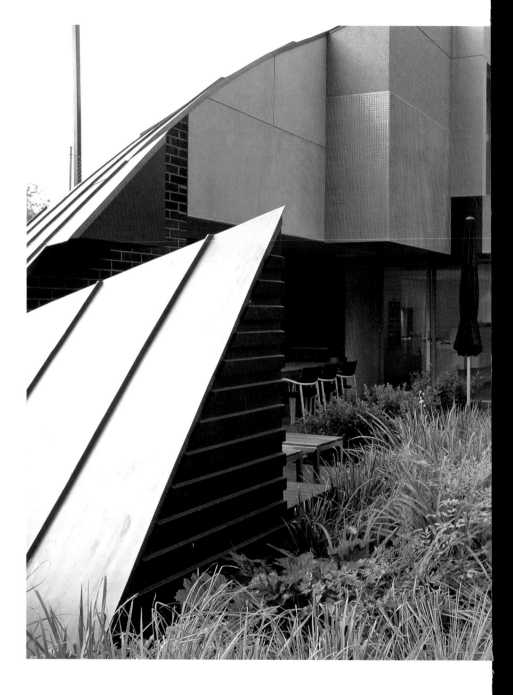

INSIDER'S TIP

Use a limited palette of plants in a variety of ways to achieve a sense of fluidity when you're standing in the house and looking at the back or front garden.

There's a pebbled terrace area for outdoor dining as well as relaxing. Although the aspect is towards the pond, it's also directed towards Boston ivy on the boundary fences. 'The colour is continually changing, from an amazing apple green to wonderful reds, and in winter, the webbing of the bare branches is striking', says Eckersley, who used Mondo grass extensively in the design. Evocative of a shag-pile carpet, it's a subtle link to the vintage of the original house.

PHOTOGRAPHY BY **Simon Griffiths**

A CLASSIC

Designed in the 1960s by Holgar & Holgar Architects, this house enjoys views to the garden via large windows and doors. While the house would have originally enjoyed a native garden, it was replaced with a European-style garden at a later stage. 'There was no relationship between the architecture and the garden. It had been filled with box hedges and urns', says landscape designer Rick Eckersley.

One of the first changes made by Eckersley was to redesign the pool and turn it into a large pond (approximately 50 square metres in area). Eckersley also added two diamond-shaped platforms to create a pontoon effect. One of the diamonds floats over the pond to allow access for feeding and viewing the goldfish. The second diamond is embedded within the pebbled pavement. To maximise the watery aspect, the pond was brought up to the edge of the living room.

Eckersley filled the pond with aquatic plants, cypressus and elephant ears, as well as pink, white and yellow water lilies. Other features of the garden are winding paths that lead from the front gate. A 'woodland' of fern-leaf maples is another essential element. 'It's important to have the sense of light and shade, moving from the coolness of the woodlands to the warmth of an open sky', says Eckersley, who was also keen to add autumnal colours in the design.

LANDSCAPE DESIGNER
Eckersley Stafford Design

DESIGNED FOR CHILDREN

This large family home was designed with a low-maintenance garden. 'Our clients have children. They wanted a garden that would be used rather than just looked at', says landscape designer Scott Leung of Eckersley Stafford Design. 'I also wanted the garden to respond to the home's strong minimal lines', he adds.

The swimming pool was located in the front garden behind a high fence because this area receives the most light. The pool and front terrace can also be viewed along the path to the front door. Framed with horsetail (a prehistoric grass), the vertical green stems create a hedge-like effect along the front path. To allow light to pass through from the front path to the pool, a glass balustrade separates the two areas. 'With the glass, you also benefit from seeing both sides of the horsetail', says Leung.

A timber deck surrounds the pool and to ensure leaves aren't continuously being fished out of the pool, there's minimal planting. A built-in bench was designed at the head of the pool for extra seating. 'At night, it's backlit, which draws light across the timber fence', says Leung. And to create privacy from neighbours, the side beds are planted with Hills weeping fig, a dense evergreen plant that creates a structured hedge.

LANDSCAPE DESIGNER **Eckersley Stafford Design**

Large glass doors feature on both sides of the open-plan living areas. This allows the front and rear garden to appear as one continuous design. The rear garden is also minimal in design. An outdoor concrete terrace is located beyond the informal meals area. This terrace joins a large turfed area. 'We used couch grass to ensure it remained green during the warmer months. It also has to withstand the children trampling', says Leung, who also ensured the turf was suitable for the father's golf practice.

The back garden also features three large peppercorn trees, which are more than 100 years old. Providing shade for the outdoor setting, they also create a leafy outlook from the kitchen and dining areas. One of the few formal plantings in the back garden is the *Buxus* balls (clipped hedges) arranged in a pebbled garden bed. Viewed from the main bedroom, this planting breaks up the hard surfacing of the terrace. 'Eventually these balls will take over the bed, adding considerable texture', says Leung.

PHOTOGRAPHY BY **Scott Leung**

INSIDER'S TIP

Working closely with clients is crucial. In this instance, the owners have three children. They wanted the design to be low-maintenance and hardy and to connect with the home's minimal lines.

ONCE A COTTAGE,
NOW A FAMILY HOME

This beachfront cottage was transformed into a family home by architect Tom Cox. A second storey was added to the house, as was a new kitchen and living area. Designed for a couple with three children, the family required a functional outdoor space. 'Previously the back garden was two lawn terraces, with the site rising 3 metres to the back fence', says landscape designer Anthony Spies.

To create two functional areas, rather than try and secure furniture to an incline, Spies removed 100 tonnes of soil. There's now one large courtyard, with a lawn area and garage above, accessed by a few stairs. Rather than replace the turf in the courtyard, Spies recycled bricks. Spies also salvaged sandstone to form the retaining walls in the courtyard. Covered in lichen and moss, these large stones create a sense of permanence in Spies' design. 'I found all the bricks and stones on a site that was being demolished. It takes years to get moss to this state', he adds.

LANDSCAPE DESIGNER **Anthony Spies Landscapes**

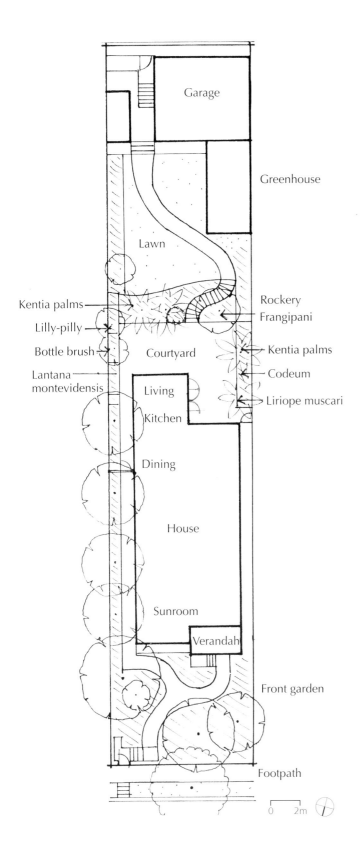

Garage

Greenhouse

Lawn

Kentia palms

Lilly-pilly

Bottle brush

Lantana montevidensis

Courtyard

Living

Kitchen

Dining

House

Sunroom

Verandah

Front garden

Footpath

Rockery
Frangipani

Kentia palms

Codeum

Liriope muscari

0   2m

The sandstone beds also provided an opportunity to bring in a whole set of new plants: ferns and palms (Kentia palms), bird of paradise and a variety of shrubs, including agapanthus and dwarfed sacred bamboo. 'These plants were ideal as the house receives the morning light. Most of the day it's in shade', says Spies.

While the garden is relatively modest in size, it's directly linked to the kitchen and living areas. And when you have the beach over the road, the only thing that's really required is a small private nook, where friends and family can catch up on the weekend. 'Part of the brief was a place for the barbeque. The owners love entertaining outdoors, particularly during the warmer months', says Spies.

PHOTOGRAPHY BY **Anthony Spies**

INSIDER'S TIP

Sometimes you have to
persevere with an idea,
even though it may appear
insurmountable at times.

MAKING THE
CONNECTION

There was no connection to the back garden from this house in a beachside suburb of Sydney. Outhouses and lean-tos closed off any view to the garden. 'It was probably best that the garden was slightly obscured', says landscape designer Anthony Spies, recalling the plastic above-ground pool that once stood in the centre of the lawn.

The house, built around 40 years ago, was renovated and its lean-tos and outbuildings were removed. Doorways were widened and bi-fold timber doors were added to link the kitchen and living areas to the outdoors. One of the first tasks for Spies was to create one level in the garden. Previously, there was a step. 'Even a small change in level can be a problem. People don't always look where they're walking', says Spies.

Clay paving stones were laid in the garden, separated with timber. Below the stained timber are water-storage tanks. 'We had to make sure air could circulate. We didn't want the water to stagnate', says Spies.

To ensure the garden could be used at all times of the year, Spies designed a timber pergola and clad the roof with translucent acrylic sheets. 'It's quite a simple structure. But it doesn't detract from the garden', says Spies. A small lawn area was also included in the garden, together with a

LANDSCAPE DESIGNER **Anthony Spies Landscapes**

water feature made of stacked slate. A brick wall rendered in a reddish colour was also added. To prevent neighbours from overlooking, the periphery of the property was planted with blueberry ash. The small evergreen tree will eventually form a hedge around the terrace.

While planting was kept to a minimum, Spies included lilly-pilly and liriope as well as dwarf day lilies. Although the garden is reasonably compact, it is large enough for the family, their three children and extended family. 'It's not uncommon to have 30 people here', says Spies, whose brief was for a highly functional garden. The new pergola also softens the home's 'harsh' façade, with the new plantings creating a softer edge around the home.

PHOTOGRAPHY BY **Anthony Spies**

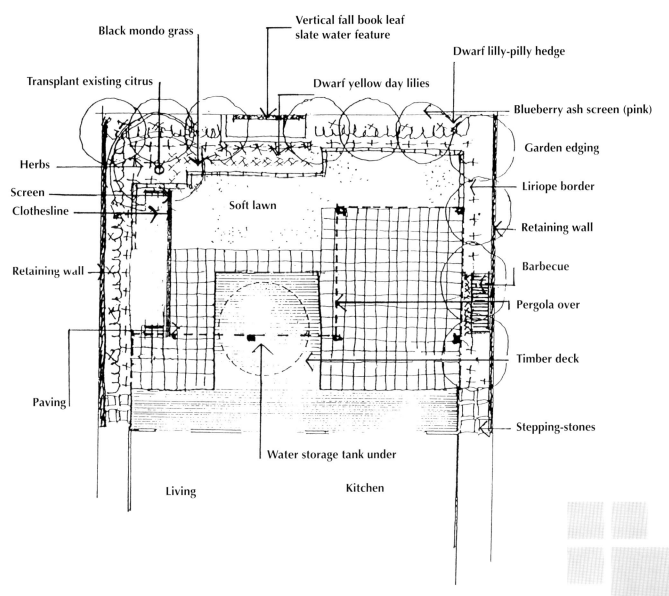

Black mondo grass

Vertical fall book leaf
slate water feature

Dwarf lilly-pilly hedge

Transplant existing citrus

Dwarf yellow day lilies

Blueberry ash screen (pink)

Garden edging

Herbs

Liriope border

Screen

Clothesline

Soft lawn

Retaining wall

Retaining wall

Barbecue

Pergola over

Timber deck

Paving

Stepping-stones

Water storage tank under

Living

Kitchen

INSIDER'S TIP

First make sure the outdoor
areas are functional, then
focus on the aesthetics and
getting the plants right.

THE FEEL OF
THE TROPICS

Designed for a semi-retired couple, this low-maintenance garden has the feel of the tropics. 'Our clients were previously living in Indonesia. They wanted the foliage to be quite rich, with a few splashes of colour', says landscape architect Perry Lethlean, a director of Taylor Cullity Lethlean.

The rendered masonry house, which features strong horizontal lines, also has strong grid-like lines in the garden. The front garden features a flagstone path embedded in pebbles. To one side of the path is a shallow pond, while on the other side is a row of camellias, each one framed in a bed the same proportions as the flagstone pavers. 'We wanted to set up a rhythm to the front door', says Lethlean.

Taylor Cullity Lethlean also inserted two small courtyards/light-wells within the house. One of the courtyards features a sculptured piece of granite that's washed over with a water feature. A few ferns line the perimeter, as does mondo grass. This courtyard can be enjoyed from the dining area. On the other side of the house is a second courtyard. Placed between the study and the home's main corridor, this courtyard provides

LANDSCAPE ARCHITECT **Taylor Cullity Lethlean**

a leafy outlook from various rooms in the house. 'It's connected to the study. The owners can walk into the courtyard or simply enjoy it from the office chair', says Lethlean, who planted taro lilies, Raphis palms and assorted ferns. A water feature in this courtyard also provides a soothing backdrop for the study.

The rear terrace garden was loosely divided into the terrace made of stone and the lap pool, framed with a toughened glass fence. 'It's not a large space. I wanted it to feel as though it was considerably more spacious', says Lethlean, who inserted one magnolia tree into the paved area.

To ensure shade all year around, Taylor Cullity Lethlean designed a protected outdoor area for alfresco dining. Made of aluminium, the canopy includes a cut-out screen wall, planted with New Zealand flaxes. 'We wanted to create a series of overlapping planes, rather than see the entire back garden at once from the living areas', says Lethlean. 'But we did want to allow the indoor and outdoor spaces to appear continuous', he adds.

PHOTOGRAPHY BY **Ben Wrigley**

INSIDER'S TIP

Designed spaces should respond to how the owners intend to use them. It is not just about creating vistas. Outdoor spaces have to be functional.

LIKE SITTING ON
THE VERANDAH

This home in Paddington, Sydney, isn't large. Only 6 metres wide, the single-fronted two-storey Victorian terrace maximises every centimetre of space, both indoors and out. 'Originally, there was no connection to the outdoors. The lean-to prevented any view from the house', says designer Debbie Pollak, who worked closely with architect Nick Tobias, director of Tobias Partners.

Tobias Partners reworked the terrace and added a new kitchen, meals area and living area to the rear of the home. To utilise every inch of space, the informal sitting area was located to one side of the home, extending to the rear boundary. Large glass sliding doors disappear into cavity walls, in both the kitchen and the elongated sitting area. When the doors are pulled back, the only things that are visible are the large steel beams. 'We wanted to open up the back courtyard as much as possible. We wanted to increase the light, as well as borrow the view of the large gum tree in a neighbour's garden', says Tobias.

Long banquette-style seating that extends from the kitchen to the rear fence includes large storage drawers. 'The lounge can be used for relaxing. It can also be used for sleeping, particularly when unexpected

ARCHITECT   **Tobias Partners Pty Ltd**

1	Laundry	6	Kitchen
2	Storage	7	Powder room
3	Courtyard	8	Formal dining
4	Banquette seating	9	Lounge room
5	Dining	10	Entry hallway

guests drop around', says Pollak, who suggested a couple of timber stools for informal eating. To strengthen the link between the kitchen and the courtyard, large concrete pavers appear in both areas. And to ensure the courtyard is used, it has been simply furnished with a steel table and bench. 'The owners have small children. The courtyard is really a place where the children can ride their bikes or simply play with their toys', says Pollak.

When the glass doors in the sitting area are pulled back, the feeling is like sitting on a verandah. Leaves blow across the courtyard and into the house, blurring the distinction between the indoors and outdoors even further. 'We could have put in a few plants. But the space is tight. And you can enjoy the greenery from the neighbour's garden', says Pollak.

PHOTOGRAPHY BY **Sharrin Rees**

INSIDER'S TIP

Think about how the space will be used. If it has to service bikes, then don't place any obstacles in their path.

THE DOWNSIZE

The owners of this house were downsizing from a large family home nearby. Rather than move into a townhouse or apartment, the owners purchased a compact corner site (approximately 600 square metres). They commissioned bg architecture to design a single-storey house surrounded with courtyards.

Designed by Adam Grundmann and Donna Brzezinski, the house is built around four courtyards. 'It's essentially a square site, so obtaining garden views from all windows wasn't too difficult', says Grundmann, who worked closely with landscape designer Jon Haughton. However, the location on a busy road did influence the design. Fortunately, the side street was lined with established oak trees and offered a more tranquil and leafy aspect.

'My first drawings of the design were C-shaped, around a courtyard. As the design progressed, so did the number of courtyards. The main courtyard leads from the kitchen. There is also a central courtyard that acts as a light well together with a courtyard leading directly from the main bedroom. And the front courtyard garden, which includes a pond, forms an interstitial space between the house and busy thoroughfare. 'The water muffles the noise from passing cars. Its presence (seen from the entrance and front study) also creates a sense of calm once you've closed the front door', says Grundmann.

ARCHITECT   **bg architecture**

The main living area is framed by garden vistas on three sides. Large timber and glass sliding doors lead directly to the paved terrace with potted plants and a jacaranda tree. While the oak trees in the street provide the main backdrop, a more intimate perspective is created with the ginger plants at ground level. The central courtyard garden is also integral to the galley-style kitchen. Apart from bringing additional light into the kitchen, this courtyard separates the main bedroom and ensuite from the second bedroom and powder room. 'Originally this courtyard was going to be a herb and vegetable garden. But it's been planted out with more decorative species', says the owner.

One of the most intimate spaces is the courtyard leading from the main bedroom. Paved in slate and featuring a built-in planter bed, it is minimally planted with bamboo. 'It's a great place to relax in. It's completely secluded. The neighbours could be miles away', says the owner, who enjoys the courtyard spaces as much as the open-plan living areas. 'We treat the courtyards like extra rooms', she adds.

PHOTOGRAPHY BY **Angus McKay and Scott Newett**

INSIDER'S TIP

Treat the courtyard spaces like outdoor rooms. Like rooms, each courtyard should provide a different function.

LOW MAINTENANCE

'Low maintenance' was the brief for this garden. 'Originally there was a 1970s house with a native garden. But the garden had become fairly unmanageable', says landscape designer Tony McLeod, who worked closely with architect Roman Franetic of Stonehaven Homes.

Previously, the path to the front door was via a small opening off the driveway. 'You weren't really aware that there was a front garden', says McLeod. A new entrance was created, with 35 steps leading to it. With this rise, McLeod was keen to create a vista to the front door. 'I saw the front garden as a resting point before you contemplate the stairs. There's also the option of meandering around the pond before you come up', he says.

The sanctuary-like, courtyard-style front garden includes purple leaf weeping maples, dwarf black pines, Hinoki cypresses and weeping ginkgo. Framing limestone paths and field granite boulders, it's a tranquil setting to wander around or enjoy from the bedroom on the ground floor as well as from the living areas on the first floor. One of the most prized vistas is gained standing at the top of the stairs and looking over the front garden towards the city skyline.

ARCHITECT
Stonehaven Homes

LANDSCAPE DESIGNER
Tony McLeod, Domain Pools & Landscapes (Vic)

McLeod also included a courtyard garden to one side of the house, adjacent to the kitchen and informal living areas. The sound of running water can be enjoyed at the edge of the terrace as well as the changing autumn leaves of the Japanese maples. 'The owners wanted to enjoy the garden without having to work in it every weekend', says McLeod.

The front garden was designed for pleasure rather than work. Central to the design is a large fishpond, surrounded by large field granite boulders. To soften the granite McLeod used a variety of plants: blue cedar, black pines and maples. Two Canadian maples were selected for their height as well as their ability to provide some shade. The ground cover includes mondo grass and Canberra turf grass, a vibrant green grass that appears like moss.

'There are some Japanese elements in the garden, but it's not a formal Japanese-style garden. It's really a hybrid', says McLeod, who used granite spouts for water features rather than traditional bamboo.

PHOTOGRAPHY BY **Patrick Redmond**

INSIDER'S TIP

Setting up a vista from within the house is crucial when designing a garden. The sight lines are as important as the sounds coming from the garden, whether it's the sound of running water or the rustle of the wind.

MINIMAL LINES

This two-storey period home couldn't be substantially altered. With an original façade, it was deemed by the local council to be of local significance. As the modest cottage wasn't suitable for a family, a large contemporary extension was added. Designed by Chris Elliott Architects, the new wing is nestled behind the pitched roof.

Landscape architect Vladimir Sitta, director of Terragram, regularly works with Elliott. 'I always work closely with Chris. The house and garden are seen as integral to each other', says Sitta. The new two-storey extension made of steel and glass has a strong connection to the garden. The kitchen and living areas overlook the rear garden, as does the main bedroom on the first floor, with a large picture window.

Sitta divided the back garden into three parts. There's a large timber deck leading directly from the living areas via glass and timber sliding doors. A 10-metre pool extends along the side of the new wing, bordered by an in situ concrete ledge on one side and a strip of pebbles on the other. The pebbles were designed as a spillway for the overflow of water. The third component is a small lawn area, simply planted with lemon-scented gum trees. While the design appears relatively simple, the 'devil' is in the detail.

ARCHITECT
Chris Elliott Architects

LANDSCAPE ARCHITECT
Terragram

A pool fence made of steel was custom-designed to allow the pool to appear relatively unbroken, as well as keeping the younger children out of the deeper end. Sitta also included an aquarium as part of the pool, creating interest for swimmers as well as those sitting in the living areas. Around the base of each gum is a small bed of pebbles, designed to ensure the lawn mower doesn't damage the trunks of the trees. 'It's not a large space, so I've tried to keep the planting quite minimal', says Sitta. And rather than fill up the garden with outdoor furniture, there's a solitary bench made of precast concrete placed on the lawn area.

In contrast to the rear garden, the front garden is relatively lush and overgrown with plants. One of the most striking aspects is the front fence, made of randomly placed timber blocks. 'I wanted the fence to look like a Japanese lantern at night. It's been lit to allow light to spill over the footpath', says Sitta.

PHOTOGRAPHY **Vladimir Sitta, Anthony Charlesworth**

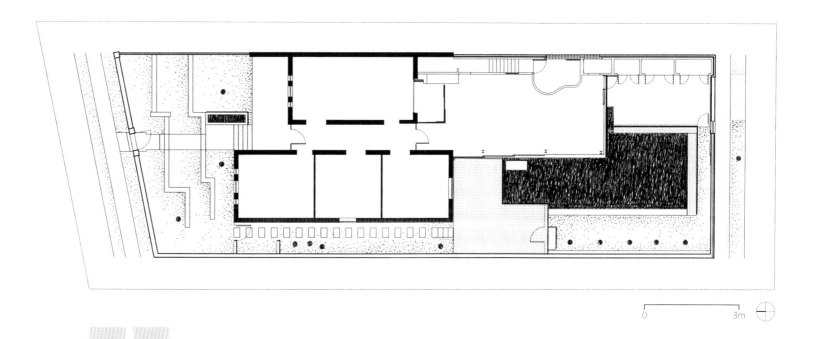

INSIDER'S TIP

It's important to connect the architecture with the landscape. The two components are integral to any brief.

A SCULPTURED LAWN

To complement this sculptural house designed by architect Luigi Rosselli it seemed appropriate to create a sculptural lawn. As the site falls steeply away from the street, this idea was achievable. 'I wanted to connect the house firmly to the landscape', says landscape architect Vladimir Sitta. And as the house is three-storey, this objective required enormous skill.

The anchoring point in Terragram's design is the rolling lawn that extends from the terrace outside the first floor to ground level, where the children's rumpus room is located. Steps are integrated into a steep grassed slope with a steel balustrade and timber handrail fixed on one side only. The pool surroundings as well as the steps are clad in Victorian bluestone. The slope has been stabilised with geotextile to prevent erosion or damage.

Apart from the pool, one of the dominant features in the back garden is a pair of mature avocado trees. Shading the rumpus room as well as the timber deck, avocado trees with twisted limbs also create a leafy vista. To ensure the children don't fall off the deck, a built-in timber bench was designed.

ARCHITECT
Luigi Rosselli

LANDSCAPE ARCHITECT
Terragram

However, while the trees are alluring, it's the pool in the back garden that draws the attention. The pool with connected channel is lined with luminous green tiles. While the large pool is used for swimming, the narrow and shallower body of water is linked to the edge of the house. And to allow people to walk rather than jump across the water, a toughened glass sheet was laid across it. Rather than carving up the water with a traditional bridge, the glass creates a contemporary layer. 'The glass is backlit. At night the effect is quite magical', says Sitta.

To one side of the lawn area is dense planting of bamboo and lilly-pilly together with ginger plants. 'I wanted to prevent overlooking from neighbours. But I also wanted light to filter through to the back garden', says Sitta.

PHOTOGRAPHY BY **Vladimir Sitta**

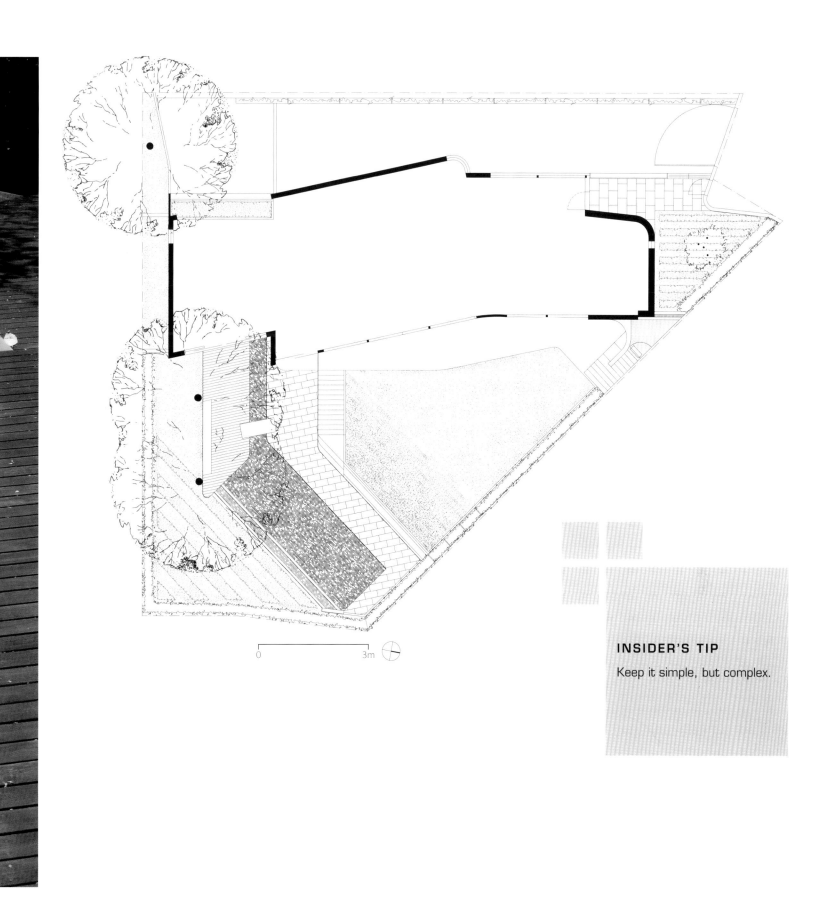

0　　　　　　　　3m

INSIDER'S TIP

Keep it simple, but complex.

ACCESSIBLE

This cottage on the banks of a river had no connection to its setting. In fairly poor condition, the house was originally surrounded with outbuildings. The few trees that had been planted blocked out the river. 'Most of the rooms were fairly enclosed', says architect Helen Rice, a director of Rice & Skinner Architects.

As the cottage was cut into the side of a hill, Rice & Skinner needed to excavate to create a larger floor plate at ground level. Corridors, both downstairs and upstairs were removed to allow for a view to the garden terraces and river. The ground floor of the house is now open plan, with double glass doors leading to the garden and deck. As the house is heritage listed, the architects were not permitted to extend the original openings, and had to replace them rather than widen them. However, new full-length glass and timber doors do allow for a more extensive view of the landscape.

One of the most used parts of the house is the large terrace, which also doubles as the main entrance to the home. Bluestone in a crazy-paving design is bordered with two garden beds. One bed features Japanese maples, while the other bed has shrubs and creepers, the latter eventually

ARCHITECT
Rice & Skinner Architects

LANDSCAPE ARCHITECT
Cath Stutterheim, Stutterheim/Anderson

spilling over new rock walls. 'Cath Stutterheim had already prepared a schematic design for our clients. We were thinking the same way in terms of the direction of the garden', says Rice. As the front terrace is also the front path, the choice was a few ceramic stools rather than a full garden setting.

The verandahs also required restoration. 'We found an original drawing of the house, which showed a return verandah', says Rice, who was able to convince the local council to allow a parking area connected to the upper level. Rice & Skinner were also able to extend the original verandah at ground level. While the increase in area is moderate, the extra space allows for an outdoor setting.

Materials used in the garden also appear in the interior. Bluestone, for example, was used on bathroom floors. 'I think it's important to create that connection, whether it's in the materials or the colours used', says Rice, who used tallow wood extensively in the living areas. 'The colour of this timber is almost the same as the river', she adds.

PHOTOGRAPHY BY **Matt Harvey**

INSIDER'S TIP

It's important to have access to a garden. Full-length glass doors not only create a visual link but also allow an immediate connection to the environment. The interior spaces feel larger as a result.

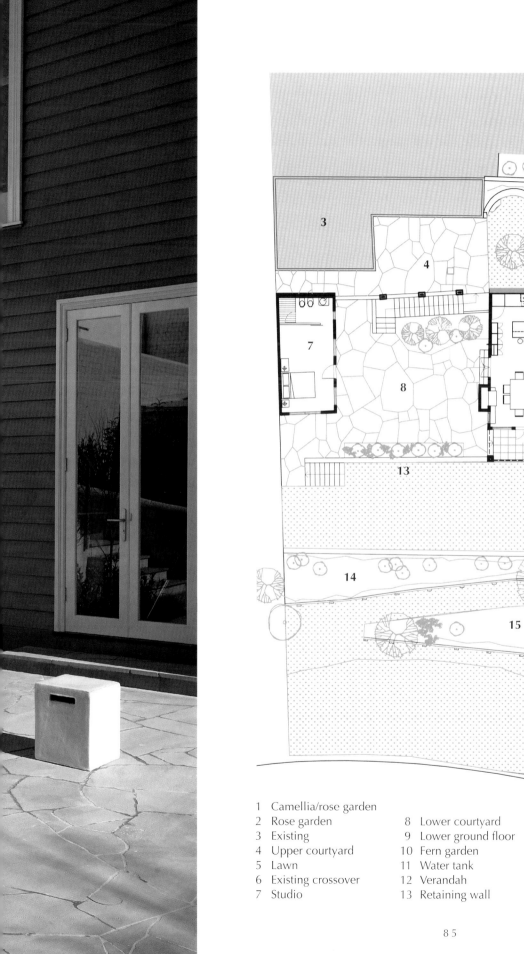

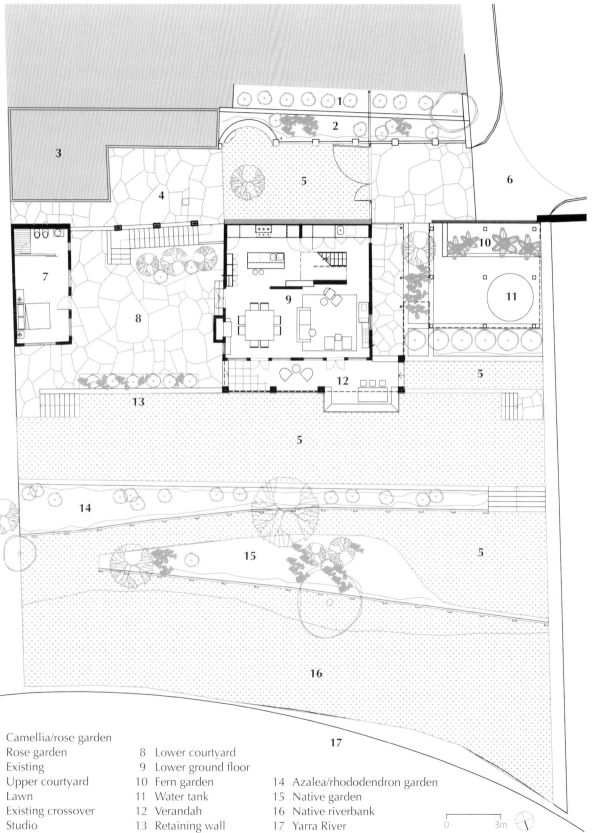

1 Camellia/rose garden
2 Rose garden   8 Lower courtyard
3 Existing   9 Lower ground floor
4 Upper courtyard   10 Fern garden   14 Azalea/rhododendron garden
5 Lawn   11 Water tank   15 Native garden
6 Existing crossover   12 Verandah   16 Native riverbank
7 Studio   13 Retaining wall   17 Yarra River

WIDENING
THE GARDEN

This semi-detached house was completely gutted by architect Peter Vernon. A second storey was added, as well as a new kitchen and living area to the rear. And with the new addition, there was a reworking of the garden. 'There were a few raised garden beds. But you had to strain your neck to see them from the original kitchen', says landscape designer Richard Unsworth, director of Garden Life.

Vernon included floor-to-ceiling aluminium and glass bi-fold doors in the new living area. A new awning made of steel was also part of the design and allows for alfresco dining. One of the main features of the garden is the sandstone day bed, with a few scattered cushions used for lying or sitting on. 'All the sandstone was found on site. It was excavated from below the house', says Unsworth. A sandstone garden bed along the rear wall, simply planted with two evergreen ash trees and some ornamental ginger plants, divides the garden from the garage. Light filters into the garage via a slatted timber wall.

Ceramic tiles were used on the flooring of the living area and extend to the small terrace that has sufficient room for a timber bench and table. To counteract the hard surfaces, a small patch of lawn was included between the sandstone day bed and garage wall. 'It's only a small patch of lawn. But it's sufficient for the owner's small children to throw a ball around', says Unsworth.

LANDSCAPE DESIGNER **Garden Life**

To extend the sense of space, Unsworth designed a pathway leading to the garage. Made of in situ concrete and mondo grass, the paving creates horizontal bands across the site. 'I didn't want to just create a hard garden path that carved up the garden. I also wanted to make sure the path could withstand traffic', he says. While the terrace-style garden is minimal in design, the side boundaries are more densely planted. Bamboo and palms appear on one side of the garden and blood grass softens a timber fence on the other side. 'I wanted to create a contrast between the foliage and the texture of the sandstone', he adds.

One of the more intimate views of the side garden can be seen every time the open-tread staircase is used. The vista through a double-height window looks towards elegant palms. With its lush aspect, this stairwell also benefits from filtered light.

PHOTOGRAPHY BY **Warwick Orme**

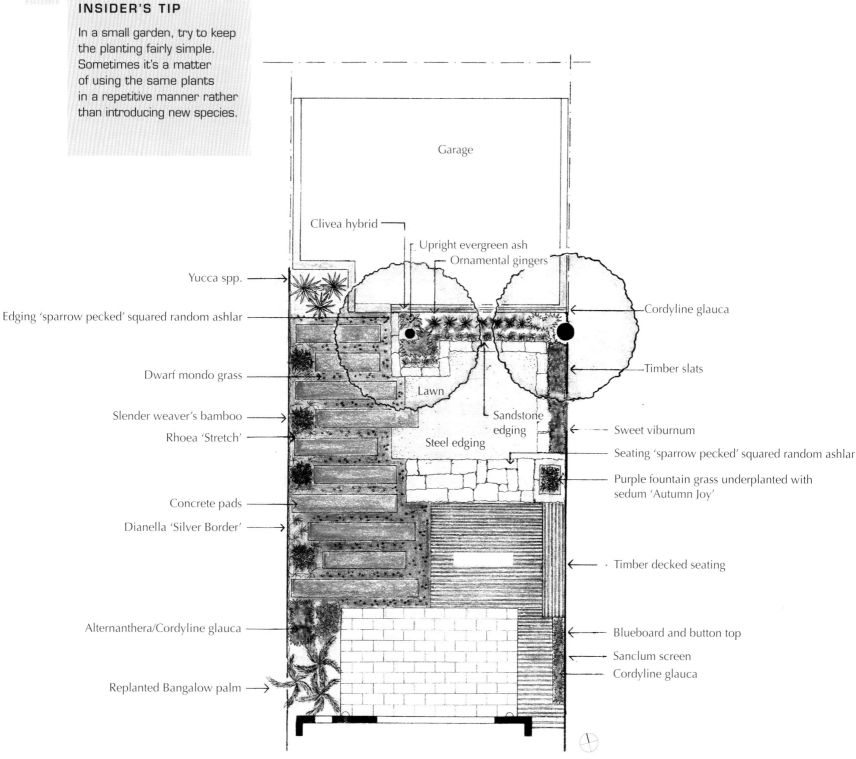

Garage

Clivea hybrid

Upright evergreen ash

Ornamental gingers

Yucca spp.

Edging 'sparrow pecked' squared random ashlar

Cordyline glauca

Dwarf mondo grass

Lawn

Timber slats

Slender weaver's bamboo

Rhoea 'Stretch'

Sandstone edging

Steel edging

Sweet viburnum

Seating 'sparrow pecked' squared random ashlar

Concrete pads

Purple fountain grass underplanted with sedum 'Autumn Joy'

Dianella 'Silver Border'

Timber decked seating

Alternanthera/Cordyline glauca

Blueboard and button top

Sanclum screen

Cordyline glauca

Replanted Bangalow palm

REMINISCENT
OF THE PAST

Landscape Architect Jane Irwin worked closely with Durbach Block Architects on this house. Both house and garden show the magic that can result when a holistic approach is taken. 'We went with the architects to inspect the site, even before anything was put to paper', says Irwin 'We both wanted to design something that was appropriate to the site', she adds.

Irwin closely examined the original garden. Located in Sydney, and overlooking the Pacific Ocean, the garden reflected many gardens from the 1950s. Rather than dismissing the garden as outdated, Irwin was captivated by its organic feel. 'There were a lot of daisy bushes and succulents, as well as ornamental grasses. Many of the plants were growing out of the stone walls', recalls Irwin.

While a few of the original plants were incorporated into a new design, the sandstone walls virtually crumbled into the ocean. New sandstone walls (varying in height from 3 metres to half a metre) were designed for the property, cascading over five levels. 'Our clients didn't want the typical parterre garden you see with many new homes. They preferred something more quirky', says Irwin, who also used dramatic colour in her scheme.

ARCHITECT
Durbach Block Architects

LANDSCAPE ARCHITECT
Jane Irwin Landscape Architecture

The task for Irwin was a difficult one. Not only did she have to deal with a multi-level garden, but also the difficult climate and windy, salt-laden air. It was also important to connect the three main openings of the house to the terrace. Each area had to be connected to the organic-shaped pool and cliff-top gardens. 'In a sense, each of the paths is a terrace and a garden. The division is quite blurred', says Irwin.

Irwin initially over-planted the garden with plants such as daisies, agave, banksias, canna lilies and white correa, together with red hot poker (*Kniphofia uvaria*) and grasses. 'I did a lot of testing of plants. I knew there would be some that wouldn't survive in these conditions', says Irwin.

One of the most dramatic landscapes is the terrace outside the bedrooms on the lowest level. Featuring sandstone walls, as well as exposed sandstone rock outcrops, the beds are both natural and man-made. 'Originally these sandstone boulders were paved over. We wanted to expose them and express them for what they were', says Irwin, who surrounded some of these stones with moss beds and smaller stones. And to create some height in this garden terrace, Pandanus trees were used.

PHOTOGRAPHY BY **Michael Wee**

INSIDER'S TIP

Study a place before you
start thinking about a
design. You shouldn't feel
constrained by traditional
styles. Each place should
have its own unique voice.

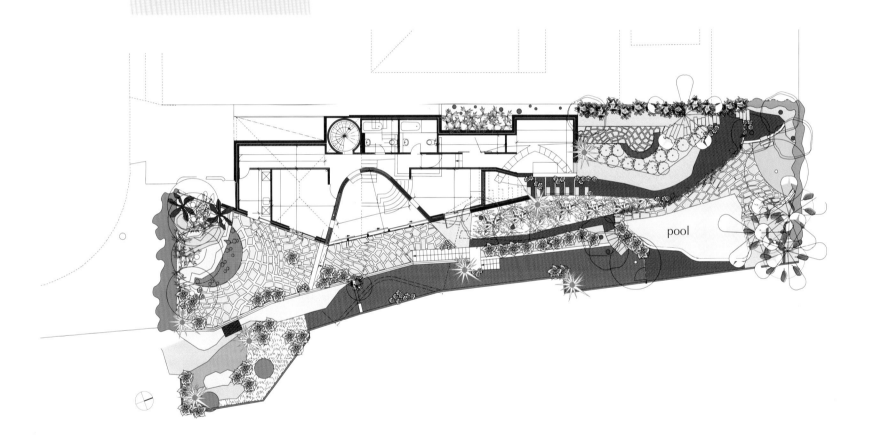

pool

AN ASIAN INFLUENCE

The owners of this 1930s home wanted an Asian-style garden. 'They didn't want a traditional garden, but something that evoked their heritage', says landscape architect Cameron Grant, director of Landarche.

While the back garden remains in fairly original condition, the front garden transforms the 1930s red brick and stucco rendered house into a contemporary setting. 'We wanted to use some of the colours and textures of the façade without being too obvious', says Grant, whose brief included a water feature and a place to sit and contemplate.

The front garden was completely reworked, with the exception of the original low brick fence and an established liquid amber abutting the front fence. Landarche designed two timber planes (supported with steel) to frame the liquid amber, placing the two at different levels. Used as a seat, the deciduous tree offers shade during summer and sunlight during winter. 'You can enjoy neighbours strolling by or focus on the water feature', says Grant, who placed an unusual water feature in the centre of the garden.

LANDSCAPE ARCHITECT   **Landarche**

Water trickles into a rock basin surrounded by black mondo grass. 'I wanted to pick up some of the textures of the home's façade', says Grant, who also included a textured granite path leading to the front door. The new driveway of exposed aggregate concrete complements the other textures in the front garden.

To ensure the front garden remained the focal point, car parking was created at the side of the house, simply protected by a timber battened carport. 'It didn't seem appropriate to create a Western-style garage. It would have been at odds with the design', says Grant.

PHOTOGRAPHY BY **Landarche**

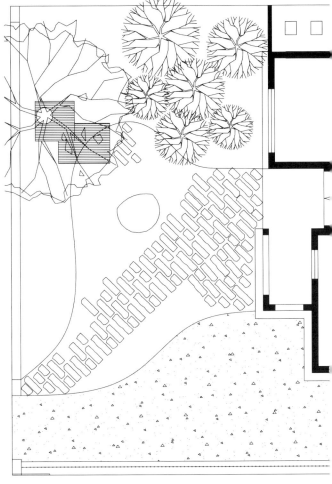

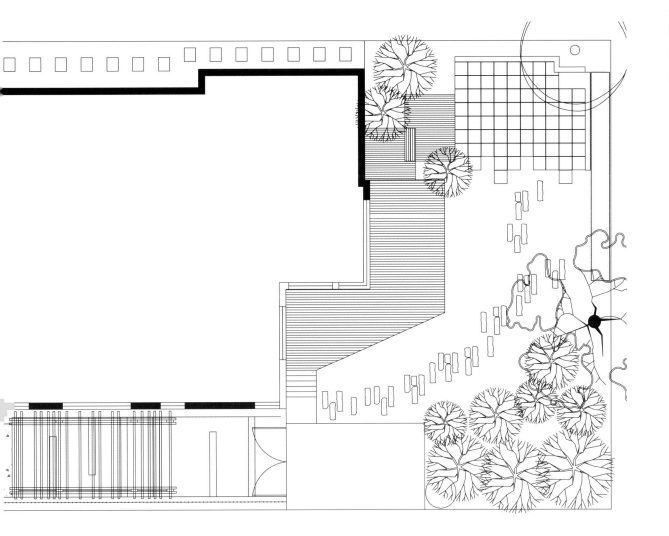

INSIDER'S TIP

Don't try to put too many ideas into the one scheme. Even if you come up with several ideas, pull back and refine the strongest ones.

A UNIQUE GARDEN

The owners wanted a unique garden that would complement their house, designed by architect Neil Clerehan. The large two-storey inner-city home occupies a significant portion of the site. But there was still sufficient room for courtyard-style gardens. 'Our clients were leaving behind an Edna Walling garden. They were looking for something similar, but in a more contemporary setting', says landscape designer Andrew Seccull, director of Jenny Smith Gardens, who worked on the garden with his partner Janet Seccull and landscape designer Luke Rabl.

The front courtyard, connected to the owner's office/study, is minimal compared to the side and rear gardens. Simply planted with a couple of Japanese maples, the garden beds feature white azaleas underplanted with native violets. Surrounded by bluestone paving, the courtyard includes a granite sculpture/water feature by Akira Takizawa. While this courtyard is enclosed with a high brick fence, there is a break in the side fence to provide a view into the rear garden.

LANDSCAPE DESIGNER   **Jenny Smith Gardens**

As the side garden is relatively narrow, the design was restricted to crushed granite stepping stones and steel mesh screens, covered with star jasmine. The screens feature a number of circular cut-outs to allow the view from the house to extend to the white-painted rendered wall. 'It's only an extra few centimetres. But it gives a sense of depth', says Andrew Seccull.

The rear garden is connected to the living areas. A small paved area includes Japanese antique temple gates. Fixed, rather than operable, these gates provide an impression that there's something beyond the rear boundary, as though there's another garden behind. 'The gates frame the space. But they also personalise the garden', says Seccull.

Also in the rear garden are two 'floating' timber decks, each surrounding maidenhair trees. Gardenias planted below create a wonderful fragrance. 'These decks were designed as day beds. It's the perfect place to relax and read the newspaper', says Seccull, who also planted the side beds with orange lilies. To the other side of the house is a flower garden, forming part of the brief. Planted with roses, there's a continual supply of fresh flowers for the house. 'The Edna Walling garden was very much about filling the house with cut flowers. We wanted to create the same experience with this garden', says Seccull.

PHOTOGRAPHY BY **Simon Griffiths**

INSIDER'S TIP

It's important to create a
sense of something beyond,
whether you're designing a
narrow side garden or a
front courtyard. Gardens can
feel private without feeling
closed in.

SUCCULENT

The owners of this 1920s timber home wanted a succulent garden. 'They had a fascination for succulent plants, so the brief headed in that direction', says landscape designer Andrew Seccull of Jenny Smith Gardens, who designed the garden with his partner Janet Seccull and landscape designer Luke Rabl.

One of the first succulents planted was a dragon tree, found by the owners in a building site that was being developed. Planted in the centre of the front garden, the tree is a focal point. 'We designed the garden beds once we knew where this tree was going to be placed', says Rabl, Creative Director at Jenny Smith Gardens.

A new metal fence was designed for the front garden, allowing unimpeded views from the front garden to the street and vice versa. New Zealand Christmas bushes appear in the garden, together with bottle trees and kangaroo paws. There's also an extensive selection of succulent plants, chosen for their colour as well as texture. 'Most of the plants are drought

LANDSCAPE DESIGNER **Jenny Smith Gardens**

resistant. It's part of their appeal', says Rabl. To eliminate the need for mowing lawns, the front garden features a series of curvaceous paths. Some of these paths are made of fine gravel, while others are constructed using a pebble from Yea in Victoria, Australia. Castlemaine slate was also used to define paths, as were timber decks. 'It's almost like a dry river bed', says Rabl.

While the garden was laid from scratch, there were a few original elements incorporated into the design. A side garden bed, made of timber sleepers, was added to the garden at some stage. The sleepers were painted a sage green to allow them to recede into the side courtyard garden, rather than dominating it. Built-in timber seats were added to this bed, fixed by rusted chains. And to create a green vista from the home's kitchen and living areas, the side garden features olive trees planted in pots.

With small children, the owners wanted a garden that was functional as well as low maintenance. The back garden contains a sand pit, a cubby house, a vegetable garden enclosed by a dry-stone wall, as well as a glasshouse for growing succulents and other species. One of the most used parts of the house is the large verandah that looks onto the side garden at the rear. 'The owners can enjoy the garden while still keeping an eye on the children', says Rabl.

PHOTOGRAPHY BY **Simon Griffiths**

INSIDER'S TIP

Create a garden that's going to be used by all members of the family. If children's needs are ignored in the design, their parents will certainly feel it.

EMPTY NESTERS

These apartments were specifically designed for empty nesters. While not quite as large as the family homes left behind, each of the three apartments enjoys either generous wrap-around balconies or, in the case of the ground floor apartment, three primary courtyards. 'It's a reasonably narrow site, so the garden spaces are relatively compact', says architect James Fitzpatrick, principal of Fitzpatrick + Partners, who worked closely with landscape company Botanica.

At the front of the ground-floor apartment is a private courtyard. A pond frames the terrace on three sides, with two concrete steps in the pond providing a connection to a small patch of grass. 'The owners of these apartments are leaving behind large gardens. They want a place outside to entertain. But they're not looking for the work associated with a garden', says Fitzpatrick. Complete with barbeque, sink and fridge, this terrace functions as an outdoor kitchen. Connected to the living and dining areas, the terrace also allows for larger groups. 'It's ideal when the extended family and friends come to visit', he adds.

Fitzpatrick and Botanica used the landscape to create divisions in the home. The main guest wing, accessed by a long corridor, looks out to a fern garden. Palms provide privacy from neighbouring properties, while

ARCHITECT
Fitzpatrick + Partners

LANDSCAPE DESIGNER
Botanica

ferns create a tropical outlook from bedrooms. Rendered planter boxes not only elevate many of the ferns, but are also filled with richer soil. 'The soil in this area has a high salt content. The ferns wouldn't have thrived if they were simply placed directly in the ground', says Fitzpatrick.

Water continues along this side courtyard. 'On warmer days, you get the moisture coming through the house', says Fitzpatrick, who included large glass window walls to strengthen the connection to the outdoor spaces. 'The sound of running water also filters through the interior spaces', he adds.

While there is also a courtyard to the rear of the ground floor apartment, the front terrace is where the owners, family and friends gravitate. Designed as an extension of the living areas, the terrace offers privacy from neighbours using the side path. 'Their time is spent around the barbeque rather than pulling up weeds', says Fitzpatrick.

PHOTOGRAPHY BY **Eric Sierins**

INSIDER'S TIP

Treat the landscape as you would treat indoor spaces. These outdoor spaces are also rooms or corridors. And like the rooms in a house, some of these spaces should be private, while others remain quite open.

MULTI-LEVEL

This house overlooking Sydney Harbour has been virtually rebuilt. Designed by Stanic Harding and featuring a garden by landscape architect Jane Irwin, there are few remnants of its past. 'There was a 1950s house on the site. We only retained a couple of walls. But you wouldn't be able to identify them', says architect Andy Harding, a co-director of the practice.

One of the problems with the original house was a lack of connection to the garden. 'It's an extremely steep sloping site. Most of the garden was unused', says Harding. With a masonry base and lightweight compressed fibro-cement cladding, the multi-level house features several courtyards. There's a front courtyard adjacent to the entrance of the home, with a small grassed area. Not visible from the street, it's only discovered once the car is parked at street level above. 'There is that element of surprise. But we also wanted to set up a variety of courtyards with various functions', says Harding.

The main courtyard leads directly from the kitchen and meals area on one side of the house. This courtyard is also connected to the formal dining and living areas. Both areas are framed by floor-to-ceiling glass stackable doors, which allow the outdoors to feel part of the interior

ARCHITECT
Stanic Harding Pty Ltd

LANDSCAPE ARCHITECT
Jane Irwin Landscape Architecture

spaces. Featuring large concrete pavers, the courtyard is simply designed with a pink frangipani tree raised in a garden bed. 'We wanted to create privacy from neighbours. But we also wanted the courtyard to function as a play area for a young child', says Harding.

Another terrace, located to the rear of the house, enjoys harbour views. Leading from the dining area, this terrace existed prior to the new home. However, the concrete terrace was resurfaced with tiles and a barbeque unit was installed, complete with a stone bench-top and plywood joinery. 'It's a wonderful place for entertaining. These water views are unparalleled', says Harding. A new timber deck was also included in the design. Located closer to the water, the deck offers yet another option to relax. Irwin has linked these terraces with winding sandstone paths. 'The paths had to be re-laid to suit the garden', says Irwin, who recycled the existing sandstone. Some palms were also reused in the design and were protected while the house was being constructed. 'We wanted the house to sit in the garden. It's an extension of the house', says Harding.

PHOTOGRAPHY BY **Paul Gosney and Andy Harding**

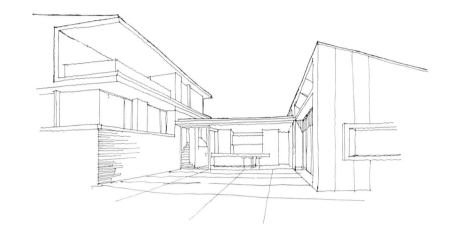

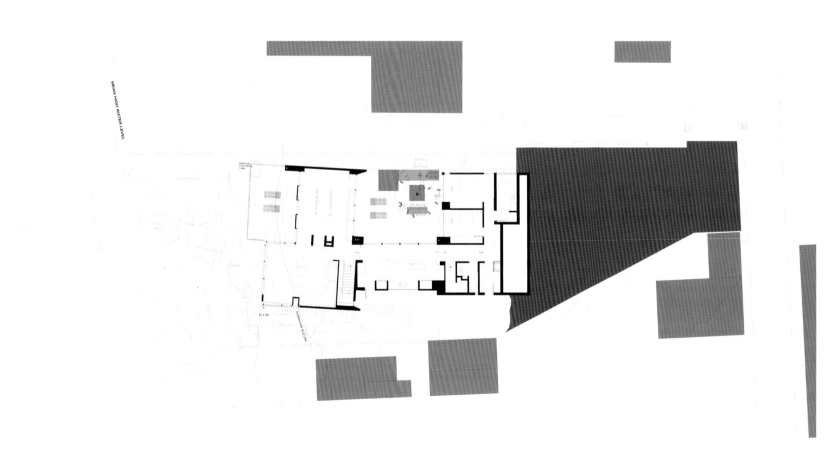

INSIDER'S TIP

You need to understand how
sunlight travels, both at
different times of the day
and also at different times of
the year. This will affect how
the garden will be used.

RECTILINEAR FORMS

The garden of this large family home follows the same strong rectilinear forms as the house. Designed by landscape architects Tract Consultants, the garden complements the two-storey house designed by Inarc Architects.

Built for a large and growing family, both the house and garden are generous in size. The open-plan casual living areas and kitchen are oriented to the rear, while the formal living areas face onto an enclosed courtyard-style garden at the front of the house. Concealed behind a high timber-battened fence, the only greenery seen from the street is a collection of honey locust trees planted equidistantly. Known for their sculptural branches, these trees feature an iridescent green leaf in summer that changes to a vibrant yellow in autumn. 'We wanted to create privacy. It's a large family and we wanted to ensure both the front and rear gardens are used', says architect Reno Rizzo, a co-director of Inarc Architects.

Inarc also created private vistas of the front garden from the children's bedrooms on the first floor. The irregular-shaped windows in these bedrooms direct the focus towards the trees rather than houses on the other side of the street.

ARCHITECT
Inarc Architects

LANDSCAPE ARCHITECT
Tract Consultants

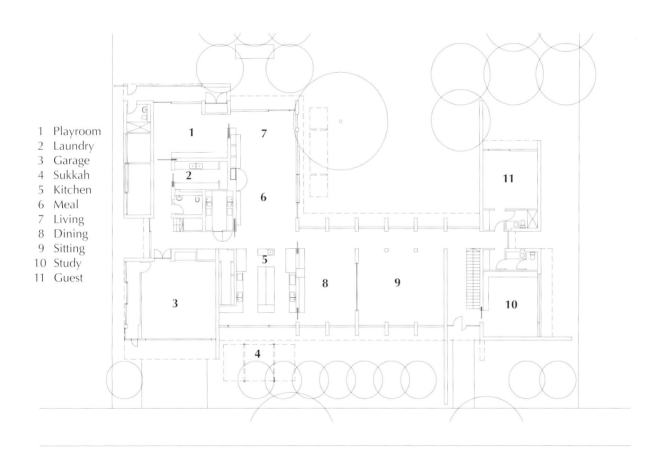

1 Playroom
2 Laundry
3 Garage
4 Sukkah
5 Kitchen
6 Meal
7 Living
8 Dining
9 Sitting
10 Study
11 Guest

Views of the back garden are considerably larger, with floor-to-ceiling glass doors leading from the informal living areas. Like the front garden, the rear garden is minimally planted. On one side of the garden is a lawn. Adjacent to the lawn is a soft rubber-like material that appears like gravel from the distance. 'We wanted to create a soft surface to insert a built-in trampoline', says Rizzo, who framed the trampoline with Chinese poplars, deciduous trees that provide sun protection throughout summer.

Also in the back garden, separated by a low rendered wall, is a swimming pool. Complete with its own 'concourse' of concrete pavers, it's an ideal retreat from playing children. And while the terrace adjacent to the pool is minimally planted with a lilly-pilly hedge, there are also automatic blinds that cover the pool during the warmer periods of the year. 'The colour used in the garden is also fairly restrained. Apart from various shades of green, the main contrast is a white star jasmine, used as ground cover', says Rizzo.

PHOTOGRAPHY BY **Peter Clarke, Latitude**

INSIDER'S TIP

It's important to see a garden from as many rooms as possible. In this house, it doesn't matter where you stand; it's there, straight in front of you.

A COMMUNAL TERRACE

Architect Dale Jones-Evans transformed this large heritage-listed woolshed into apartments. As there was no space at ground level to create gardens, the rooftop was appropriated. 'The building was gutted in the late 1980s. It was converted into a car park, including the rooftop', says Jones-Evans, who worked with architects Marchese + Partners and with 360°. 'Being on the edge of the city, it seemed appropriate to provide a large communal terrace (200 metres by 40 metres)', he adds.

'Our design responded to limited outdoor private space, due to heritage issues. Our clients wanted to create an unexpected rooftop landscape, an island in the sky. It's a green roof that's accessible and functional for all residents and one that makes a positive ecological contribution to the urban environment', says landscape architect Daniel Baffsky, Principal of 360°.

Spread over two levels (6 and 7), the terraces include a sea of native grasses, a mature dragon's blood tree and several elevated decks linked by angular paths. Recycled decorative mulches including concrete and terracotta roof tiles, in vibrant ochre, feature in some of the garden beds. 'The design of the rooftop was pragmatically driven. The plants had to withstand fairly hostile conditions', says Baffsky, who included fluid concrete planters in the design.

ARCHITECT
Dale Jones-Evans and Marchese + Partners

LANDSCAPE ARCHITECT
360°

One of the most used parts of the roof garden is the grassed area, with small pockets of lawn randomly dispersed in between. 'When you're sitting down on the lawn, you feel as though you're miles away. It's only when you stand up that you take in the city vista', says Baffsky.

All residents have access to the garden, via a lift that leads to a timber-battened walkway. 'The garden wasn't designed as one vista. The idea is to discover new things about it all the time', says designer Liam Noble of 360°, who was inspired by post-war modernist gardens from Brazil. 'There's also a sculptural playfulness about the space, particularly on Level 7', says Baffsky, referring to the organic shaped paths that meander through the garden. And as the depth of the garden beds is limited due to being on a roof, many of the trees, such as the tuckeroos, a native plant from the east coast of Australia, are planted in raised concrete beds.

PHOTOGRAPHY BY **John Gollings**

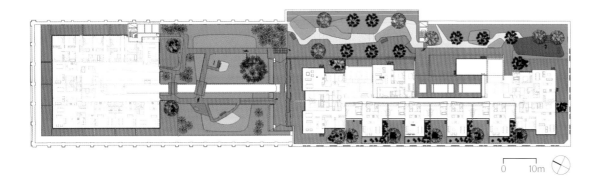

INSIDER'S TIP

Remain focused on your primary objective and create a useable space that can be enjoyed by all.

PARED BACK

The owners of this house had outgrown their original 1930s home on the same site. However, there was sufficient land at the rear of the property to create a contemporary new wing. And unlike the 1930s house that faces a busy thoroughfare, the side street the property abuts is relatively quiet.

While the brief for the new wing and garden was reasonably loose, a few key words were given to the architect Greg Gong. 'I think one of the words we used was "dramatic"', says the owner, who like Gong, was raised in China. 'We both relate to the very simple homes you see in China. There's a wonderful relationship between the indoor and outdoor spaces', says Gong.

The new wing covers nearly 290 square metres of land, with the original house now used as a guest wing. Set back 6 metres from the side street, a minimally planted courtyard is the main outdoor space. 'The family have a busy schedule. The brief included a low-maintenance design, both for the house and garden', says Gong, who included bluestone floors for the kitchen and living areas, as well as for the courtyard.

ARCHITECT **Greg Gong**

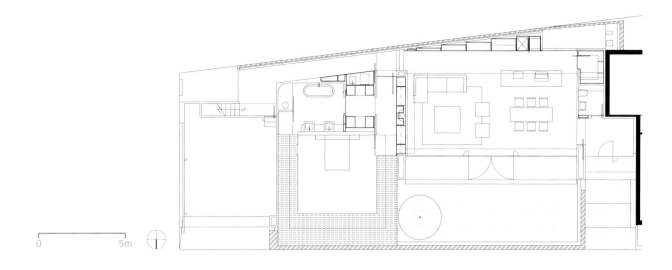

0   5m

Although the main living areas create a sense of drama, there's a quieter story around the corner that includes the main bedroom, dressing area and ensuite. Framed on three sides by glass and surrounded by a pond, with goldfish and water lilies, there's a sense of tranquillity upon entering this zone. 'In China, this area is referred to as a half pavilion. The water creates a sense of calm', says Gong. At first the owners felt a little uncomfortable with the level of exposure to the bedroom. However, there is a high brick fence, as well as two further layers of cover, one being blinds, the other hand-drawn curtains.

And although the main bedroom feels exposed, a stainless steel cantilevered blade roof provides protection from the sun. Gong also thought about what type of tree would offer shade in the warmer months. One solitary Chinese scholar tree was carefully positioned in the courtyard that leads from the living areas. Gong speaks of the tree in the same way he describes architectural details. 'This tree has translucent lime-green leaves. You can almost see through them. And it's positioned to throw just enough shade to the bedroom.'

Gong also included a small courtyard adjacent to the kitchen. A frameless glass window adjacent to the kitchen pantry is in fact a sliding door. Relatively small in size, this courtyard functions as a clothes-drying area. 'I wanted to keep the main courtyard free of clothes. It's a place to relax, not to work in', says Gong, who was keen to keep the design of the courtyard as pared back as possible.

PHOTOGRAPHY BY **Shannon McGrath**

INSIDER'S TIP

Sometimes it's best to keep things simple. It's not just about appealing to the visual senses; it's also about being in tune with the aural senses. The sound of moving water can have as strong an impact as the sight of a garden full of plants.

THREE USEABLE AREAS

This Californian Bungalow originally had no useable outdoor spaces. A carport in the front garden used most of the space and what was left over was difficult to access. There was little joy in the back garden, with sloping land making it almost impossible to use. For a family with two children, both the house and garden needed serious attention.

Stanic Harding completely remodelled the house, adding on a two-storey addition to the rear. Outside, they worked with landscape designers Spirit Level Designs so that the house, both at the front and rear, now connects to the garden.

The carport was removed from the street frontage and a new terrace with timber battened wall was added. Concrete tiles were laid and a new garden bed was designed, planted with Ctenanthe (grey star), Indian hawthorn and philodendron. 'The ctenanthe grow to about 800 millimeres in height, so they create the privacy you require in a front garden', says Hugh Main of Spirit Level Designs.

The original narrow front balcony was also redesigned. 'We also extended the balcony by 1 metre to allow sufficient room for an outdoor setting', says architect Andrew Stanic, co-director of the practice. A timber

ARCHITECT
Stanic Harding Pty Ltd

LANDSCAPE DESIGNER
Spirit Level Designs

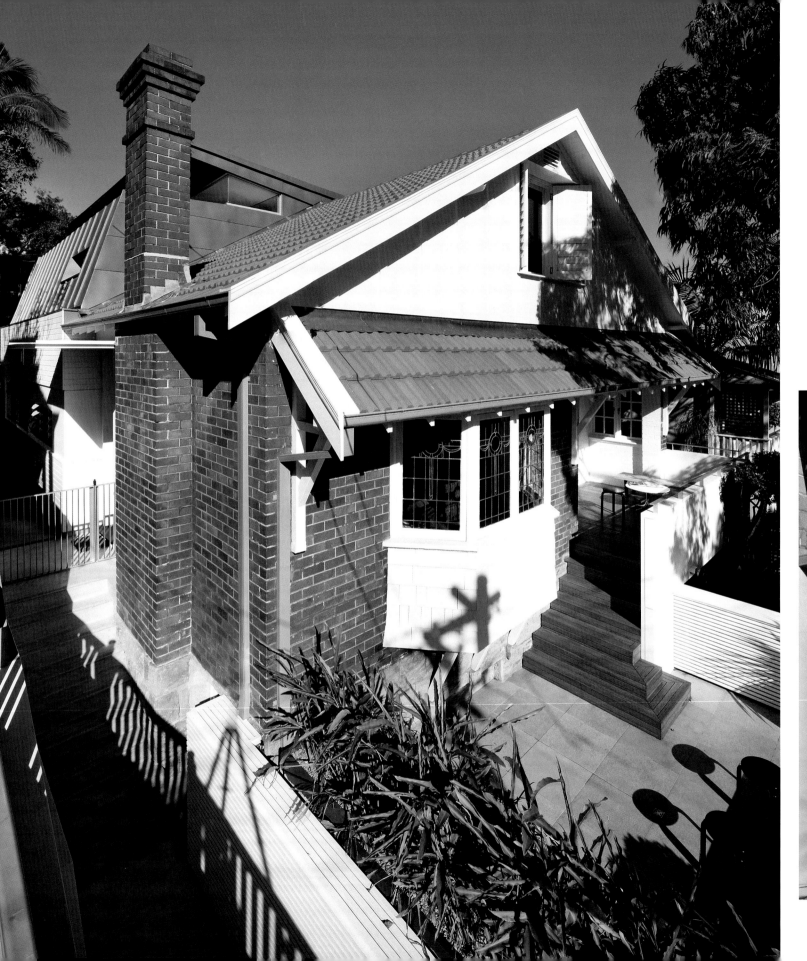

staircase, which connects to the timber deck on the balcony, was added to further ensure the front balcony and terrace were functional.

One of the greatest improvements has been in the back garden. Two levels were created. A timber deck on the lower level extends across the kitchen and informal living areas. A new set of concrete steps links the deck to a lawn area. And a sandstone drystone wall frames the garden. A built-in timber seat was also included in the design to allow the garden to be used more frequently. Like the zinc-clad extension, concrete stairs to the garden are sculptural in form. 'We wanted the house and garden to feel connected', says Stanic. 'And we wanted the outdoor spaces to be used, not just admired from the house', he adds.

PHOTOGRAPHY BY **Paul Gosney Photography and Andy Harding**

INSIDER'S TIP

Make sure the outdoor spaces are accessible. And if you're thinking of using a front garden, ensure there's a high level of privacy.

1	Awning	7	Store
2	Entry	8	Dining
3	Planter	9	Study/guest
4	Front terrace	10	Bathroom
5	Living	11	Playroom
6	Kitchen	12	Rear garden

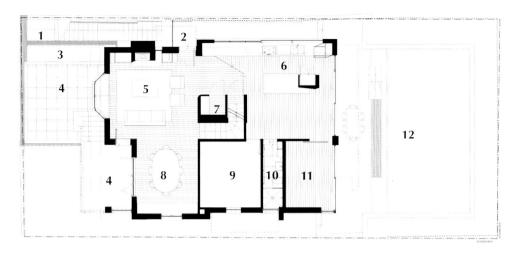

A JAPANESE FEEL

This 1970s house originally had little connection to the garden. With several oddly placed doors and windows, it was difficult to find the entrance to the home, as well as the door to the rear garden. A street tree with a developed root system was also creating havoc in the front garden. 'The roots were uplifting the bluestone paving', says Stuart Griffiths, who redesigned the garden and made new openings in the house.

One of the largest changes was in the front garden (the rear garden was essentially unchanged as it's a play area for the owner's two young children). Two large antique Chinese gates were installed. These open to reveal large bluestone pavers that lead directly to the front door. Framed with mondo grass, these pavers act as a welcome mat. Two red-stemmed Japanese maples also border the front door. 'I wanted to create a Japanese-style garden, but with a more contemporary feel', says Griffiths, who worked with Susan Burns in selecting the plants and James Stirton in creating the design.

LANDSCAPE DESIGNER   **Natural Style Landscaping**

The front garden, divided by the bluestone path, is essentially two courtyard-style spaces. On one side of the front garden is a terrace with bluestone, laid in a random design. This terrace is bordered with a garden bed, planted with New Zealand rock lilies, irises, gardenias and hellebores. At night this garden bed is externally lit and during the day it's rich in colour.

On the opposite side of the garden path, also in the front garden, is a raised timber deck. Leading directly from the dining and living areas, this terrace functions as an outdoor room. Griffiths included a sunken table (500 millimetres deep) in the deck. Complete with large Japanese-style cushions, this table is ideal for outdoor dining. Minimally planted with a few maples, it's accessible via floor-to-ceiling timber and glass doors. 'It's really another living space and it's usually quiet', says Griffiths, pointing out the children's playground in the back garden.

PHOTOGRAPHY BY **Robert Churchus of in2uitionphotography**

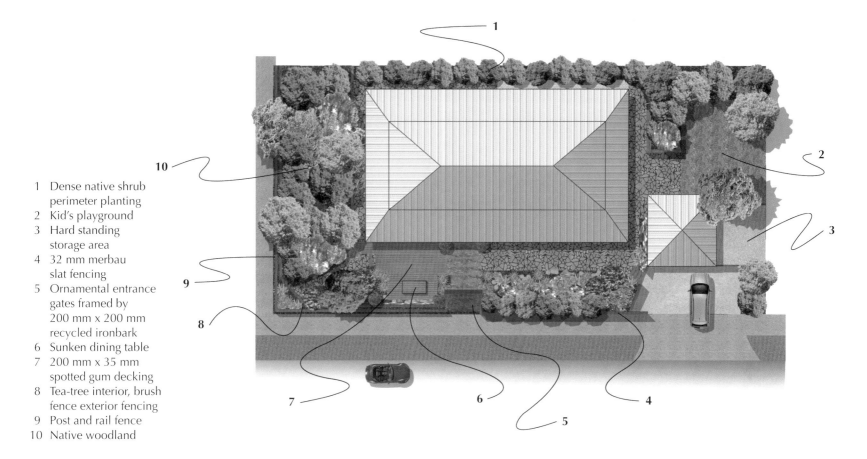

1. Dense native shrub perimeter planting
2. Kid's playground
3. Hard standing storage area
4. 32 mm merbau slat fencing
5. Ornamental entrance gates framed by 200 mm x 200 mm recycled ironbark
6. Sunken dining table
7. 200 mm x 35 mm spotted gum decking
8. Tea-tree interior, brush fence exterior fencing
9. Post and rail fence
10. Native woodland

INSIDER'S TIP

Think about how the outdoor spaces are going to be used. If you want to create a tranquil environment, there's no point in putting a children's sandpit in the same space.

ON THE EDGE
OF THE POOL

This terrace is on the edge of a pool. Separated by a toughened glass balustrade, the pool is integral to the open-plan living areas. Accessed via stackable glass doors, the terrace doubles as an outdoor eating area. 'It comfortably holds a table to seat 10 to 12 people', says architect Peter Williams, a director of Williams Boag Architects.

Originally a Victorian house, there was unsightly 1970s addition. The house was extensively renovated and a new kitchen, dining and living area were added. To delineate the past from the present, the architects used concrete flooring as opposed to timber (in the Victorian portion). The concrete floor used in the dining area also extends to the terrace.

A 1970s pool was retained in the design. But it has been resurfaced and designed to allow the water to flow beneath the concrete terrace. 'You feel as though you're sitting on the edge of the pool, whether you're around the dining table or on the terrace', says Williams.

The pool does encroach on most of the backyard. However, there is a raised garden bed on one side and a winding path of recycled bricks on the other. 'We reused the 1970s bricks', says Williams, who also included a timber-slatted screen in the garden to conceal pool equipment and a hot water service.

ARCHITECT   **Williams Boag Architects**

One of the most appealing aspects of the garden can be seen from the main bedroom, through a new box-bay window. 'It's great lying in bed and looking at the water. It appears to extend indefinitely', says Williams.

A relatively compact garden, the terrace functions as another room. 'It's quite a tight site. But the curvature of the pool makes the garden feel considerably wider. And you're conscious of it (the garden) even when you're standing at the kitchen bench', says Williams.

PHOTOGRAPHY BY **Peter Dunphy**

INSIDER'S TIP

It's important to connect as many rooms to the garden as possible. Even a glimpse of a garden bed or the swimming pool extends the sense of space in a house.

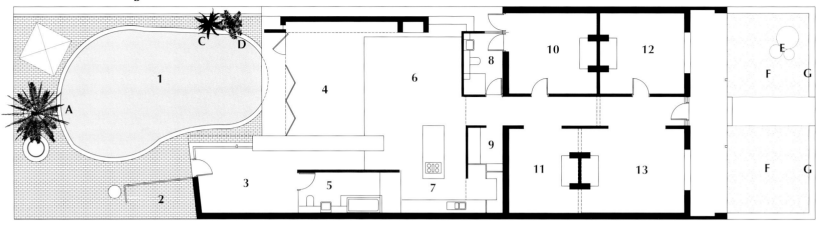

Building
1 Pool
2 Plant store
3 Bedroom
4 Dining room
5 Ensuite
6 Living
7 Kitchen
8 Bathroom
9 Laundry
10 Existing bedroom
11 Existing reception
12 Existing study
13 Existing reception

Landscape
A Bangalow palm
B Tiger grass
C Strelitzia
D Flax
E Sculpture
F Grass land
G High courtyard wall

ANOTHER ROOM

A fig vine conceals the façade of this 1920s home. Unlike its neighbours, predominantly Victorian cottages, this home could be mistaken for a garden. 'There was nothing I particularly liked about the style of the original home, or its garden. It certainly wasn't its orientation (away from the sun). The only thing going for it was the depth of the site (50 metres)', says architect Stephen Jolson, who renovated this home for himself.

Although the backyard was generous, its dimensions couldn't be appreciated from the house. A caravan, doubling as an extra room, was plonked just outside the back door. 'There was no connection to the garden at all. The only sense of greenery was the fig vine meandering across the front window. As Jolson converted the front room into a home theatre, the vine proved ideal for creating a veil to the sunlight.

To connect the garden to the bedroom and living areas, Jolson created an internal courtyard. He used what was once the back garden to create a main bedroom suite, including a walk-in dressing area. The main bedroom now has filtered views of the courtyard through a laser-cut steel screen on one side and an angled recycled water wall on the other. 'Looking through the water you feel as though you're in a grotto. It has that tropical feel',

ARCHITECT   **Stephen Jolson Architect**

INSIDER'S TIP

Keep the spaces fairly simple and select plants that create interest at different times of the year. The robinia captures the seasons perfectly.

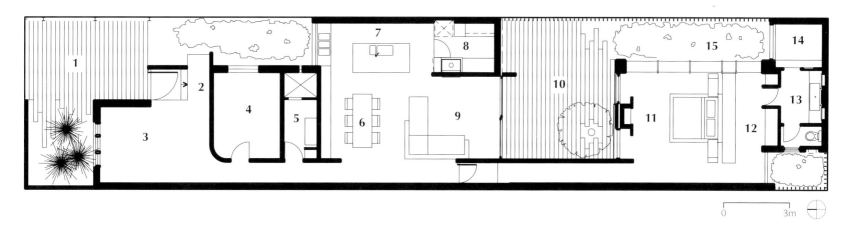

says Jolson, who extensively planted Timor black bamboo on the periphery. 'At night the garden lights create watery shadows on the ceiling.' The connection to the garden from the ensuite is as unique. Jolson included a sunken bath with a glass pivotal door. When this door is left open, there's a sense of showering outdoors in the bamboo.

The view to the courtyard from the kitchen and living areas is considerably sharper than from the bedroom. Floor-to-ceiling glass doors in the living area disappear completely into cavity walls to allow a transition between indoors and outdoors. And to create a seamless connection between the living areas and courtyard, timber floors feature in both areas. Apart from a few pots bought on travels to India, the main focus of the courtyard is a robinia tree. Its leaves turn a golden yellow in autumn and provide a lush canopy during the warmer months. 'It's quite a meditative courtyard. Particularly when the water wall is operating. You really could be anywhere in Asia', says Jolson.

1   Carport
2   Entry
3   Home theatre/study
4   Bedroom 2
5   Powder room/bathroom 2
6   Dining
7   Kitchen
8   Laundry
9   Lounge
10 Courtyard
11 Master bedroom
12 Dressing room
13 Master ensuite
14 Shower/spa
15 Water feature

A 20 PERCENT SLOPE

These three-storey townhouses in Brisbane have a similar typology to terrace-style homes. Long and narrow, the seven homes sit on a relatively compact and steep terrain. While the 20 percent slope created a challenge for the architects, it provided the opportunity for basement car parking. A common entrance was designed for the seven homes, with the front entrance of the property resembling a driveway to a single house. 'We didn't want the garages to be prominent to the street', says architect Shaun Lockyer, a director of Arkhefield, who worked closely with landscape architect John Mongard.

Rather than create a blank wall to the street, the designers have put a raised bed in front of the front fence. A water feature, framed with birds of paradise plants, provides a welcome mat for both owners and visitors.

A communal courtyard garden on the first level is also welcoming. Poincianas trees at basement level pierce through the first floor of the development and frame an elevated pond. 'The poincianas trees are native to Queensland. They're an ideal tree for shading and they produce the most wonderful red flowers in spring', says Lockyer, who surrounded the pond with toughened clear glass. A central garden bed in the courtyard is raised above the tiled terrace, which also includes a spa. 'This area receives the most sun, so it's an ideal place for residents to catch up', he adds.

ARCHITECT
Arkhefield

LANDSCAPE ARCHITECT
John Mongard

INSIDER'S TIP

It's important in a development like this to create a level of privacy without the sense of feeling hemmed in. It's also important to create the right mixture of private and communal spaces.

Private terraces were also created adjacent to the communal courtyard. These light-filled spaces have individual plywood awnings for protection from both the sun and rain. And to the rear of each home is another terrace, leading directly from the kitchen and living areas. 'We had to excavate into the site to create these terraces', says Lockyer, who was also required to screen the retaining wall behind. A timber-battened screen, made of spotted gum, is combined with a dense planting of birds of paradise. 'The idea was to create a sense of something beyond, even though the property finishes here', says Lockyer, who used the bedrooms above to create a canopy for the rear terrace.

PHOTOGRAPHY BY **Scott Burrows, Aperture Architectural Photography**

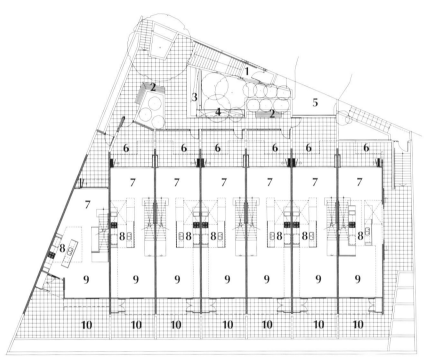

1 Entry canopy
2 Timber seat
3 Water feature
4 Cascade water feature
5 Driveway below
6 Terrace
7 Dining area
8 Kitchen
9 Family area
10 Courtyard

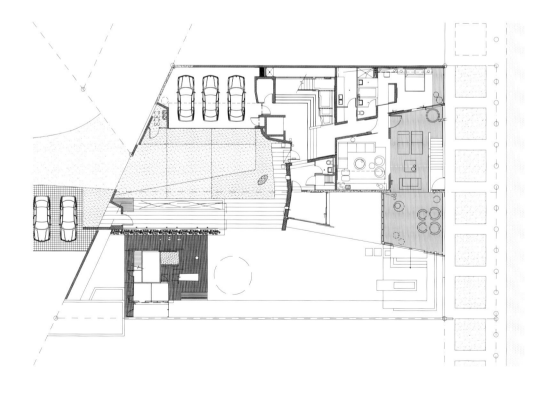

A NUMBER OF EXPERIENCES

This large home, overlooking the Brisbane River, has several terraces, each of which create different experiences. Designed by Arkhefield, in conjunction with landscape architect Jonathan Weinert, there are spectacular views of the city as well as more intimate views of the garden.

Designed for a couple with six children, the diversity of both outdoor and indoor spaces is extensive. 'The children range from young children, to teenagers, to young adults. There was no point in creating one large playground for all of them', says architect Shaun Lockyer, a director of Arkhefield.

One of the most memorable outdoor spaces is the side garden. Featuring a fire pit as well as a built-in limestone seat, there's a sense of occasion. 'It's a great space at night. The summer months can get extremely hot. But the evenings can be quite pleasant, particularly if the fire is going', says Lockyer. Limestone was used for the steps leading to a semi-enclosed outdoor terrace. Framed with tallow wood timber-battened walls, this space is light filled and out of the direct rays of the sun. A built-in lounge and large tub chairs create the sense of a room rather than an outdoor terrace. Leading from a casual living area, this terrace also provides extra space for larger gatherings.

ARCHITECT
Arkhefield

LANDSCAPE ARCHITECT
Jonathon Weinert

INSIDER'S TIP

It's important to create several different experiences. It's not just about looking at the river. There's the city as well a variety of garden vistas to engage with.

Arkhefield also designed a large terrace on the first floor, leading from the formal living areas. With built-in fireplace and seating, it's a magical space for both adults and children. A battened timber wall, also made from tallow wood, includes a window/screen. 'We wanted to include a view of the city skyline as well as keep out the harsh afternoon sun', says Lockyer.

One of the most used terraces of this house leads directly from the informal meals area. This terrace contains a plunge pool, and unlike the other terraces, is open to the sky. 'It's a fairly robust garden. The planting has been kept to a minimum', says Lockyer, referring to the bamboo, xanthorrea (a spiky-leafed plant) and the pandanus trees planted at the front of the house.

PHOTOGRAPHY BY **Scott Burrows, Aperture Architectural Photography**

A COMMUNITY

Living in some apartments can feel isolating. With no connection to a garden, except local parks, there's a sense of being cut off from the wider community. Apartments designed by architects DesignInc and landscape architects Landarche serve to bring the outdoors in. 'The brief included creating a sustainable garden, with as much natural light getting into the apartments and terrace areas as possible', says landscape architect Gameron Grant, a director of Landarche.

The development includes four residential towers; the rear towers are nine-storey, while the front buildings extend to five. 'We were fortunate to be able to start with a blank canvas', says Grant, who inherited a car park and a few derelict buildings. Stormwater runoff is channelled into garden beds and bio-retention swales bound by rocks allow water to infiltrate water tables. Landarche also incorporated recycled materials in its design, using timber cubes and benches. 'We looked at the communal spaces. We wanted to create a sense of intimacy, but also a degree of spaciousness', says Grant.

ARCHITECT
DesignInc

LANDSCAPE ARCHITECT
Landarche

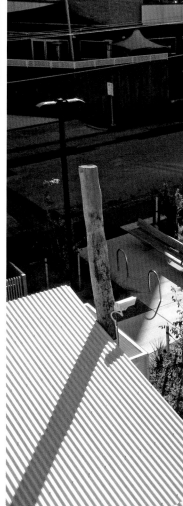

To reduce the amount of water needed for the gardens, Landarche used a selection of drought-resistant species: long-leafed flax, running postman, maidenhair creepers, crepe myrtle and deciduous maples. To the rear of the property, when natural sunlight is diminished, there is a generous bed of giant timber bamboo. 'It's quite a cool and moist environment, ideal in summer when it's just too hot to sit outside', says Grant.

However, the central courtyards between the two sets of apartments are used for most of the year. Ideal for meeting up with friends, these spaces include bike racks and generous paved areas lined with precast concrete.

PHOTOGRAPHY BY **Landarche**

1 Building 1
2 Building 2
3 Building 3
4 Building 4
5 Water tank
6 Wastewater treatment plant room
7 Pre-treatment tank
8 Post-treatment tank

0   10m

INSIDER'S TIP

Use deciduous trees to achieve shade in summer and sun in winter. You will also benefit from the rich colour of the changing leaves. It's important to create areas where people can be outdoors, while not in the path of the direct sun.

SHATTERED

This garden, designed by landscape artist by Mel Ogden, looks shattered. Granite blocks of varying sizes appear to have come loose from the paved courtyard to the rear of the house. 'I wanted to create a holistic vision for the client, one in which the garden connects to the architecture', says Ogden, who worked with Rice + Skinner Architects.

The inner-city terrace was completely reworked by Rice + Skinner. A new contemporary kitchen and living area was added to the rear, with full-length steel and glass doors. A Juliet-style balcony, with an iron balustrade, allows the garden to be enjoyed from the first level. The brief for the interior as well the garden was for a contemporary design, one that reflected the owner's collection of contemporary art.

Using Harcourt granite blocks in a number of sizes (from blocks of 1 cubic metre to 50-centimetre blocks), Ogden 'fragmented the garden'. A paved terrace leads from the living areas and is used for outdoor dining, but appears to dissolve into a pond. 'I wanted the garden to feel as though it had been slightly shattered', says Ogden, who continued the water along the side of the house. 'Normally these areas are difficult to get to. And they're quite dark. This way the water can be enjoyed from all the living areas', she adds.

ARCHITECT
Rice + Skinner Architects

LANDSCAPE DESIGNER
Mel Ogden

Ogden kept the planting to a minimum. A Japanese maple in an elevated granite garden bed loosely separates the paved area from the pond. Low alpine plants surrounding the maple also appear on a number of the floating granite blocks. 'It's a fairly low-maintenance garden. The courtyard also doubles as off-street parking', says Odgen, pointing out the timber gates and fence screening the garden from the laneway.

However, as the car is generally parked in the street, the main focus of the garden is the water. 'It's quite a meditative environment. It also takes on an abstract appearance from the bedrooms on the first floor', says Ogden.

PHOTOGRAPHY BY **Emma Cross**

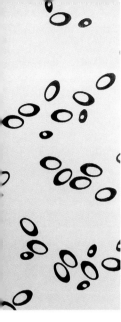

ANIMATED WALLS

This inner-city apartment benefited from a terrace down one side of the house. However, on the other side, there was only a narrow sliver of land, with bedroom windows and bathrooms forced to look towards a blank wall.

Approximately 700 millimetres wide by 17 metres long, the narrow strip provided an opportunity as well as a constraint. 'I didn't want the owners to feel as though they were hemmed in by neighbours', says designer Mel Odgen, who used a neighbouring party wall to create an inspiring contemporary garden.

LANDSCAPE DESIGNER   **Mel Ogden**

As the owners of the apartment have two cats, Ogden used this as a starting point. Reflective vinyl was attached to the wall in a silvery-grey colour to reflect natural light back into the bedrooms. The vinyl was also adorned with bubble-like shapes in bright red that resemble cat's eyes. 'The wall glows at night in a similar manner to a road sign', says Ogden, who used minimal planting in the garden bed to allow for low maintenance. Granite boulders and fine pebbles are interspersed with native grasses.

From the interior, the 'eyes' could be mistaken for bubbles, with the wall creating a fish-tank-like feel. And although it's only a narrow garden, floor-to-ceiling windows in the bedrooms increase its presence.

PHOTOGRAPHY BY **Emma Cross**

INSIDER'S TIP

You need to have a visual and tactile flow between the interior and exterior spaces. It's important to get an appreciation of the whole composition.

1 Nature strip
2 Footpath
3 Garden
4 Porch
5 Bedroom
6 Courtyard
7 Bathroom
8 Laundry
9 Living
10 Kitchen
11 Dining

0   4m

AN OUTDOOR ROOM

This single-storey terrace home was left vacant for years before the current owner moved in. Completely run down, the house had rotten floorboards on the inside and cracked concrete on the outside. Redesigned by architect Stephen Varady, the original front rooms were retained, while a new two-storey wing was added to the rear.

On a relatively small site, approximately 160 square metres, one of the main issues was getting light into the core of the building. To achieve this, a new courtyard was added, located between the living areas and a study/fourth bedroom. When the glass doors are pulled back, there's a direct link from the courtyard all the way to the rear garden. Varady kept the planting in the courtyard to a minimum to ensure it was used. Apart from a few potted plants and a Japanese maple, there's only a built-in timber bench.

The rear courtyard is also fairly sparse. A patch of lawn and a concrete paved terrace comprise the entire garden. To ensure that the courtyard was enjoyed from the upstairs as well as from the kitchen, the corridor leading to the two upstairs bedrooms features a toughened glass floor. 'We wanted to get as much light into the house as possible, while still allowing for privacy', says Varady.

ARCHITECT   **Stephen Varady Architecture**

As the house benefits from access to a rear street, Varady created a second 'frontage' to the rear. A garage door, made of powder-coated steel, has angled louvres. Those passing by can look into the rear garden, yet are restricted from looking into the house. 'We didn't want to treat the rear façade like a laneway. It's part of the streetscape', says Varady, who also planted native grasses above the concrete beam that supports the garage door. A built-in watering system allows the grasses to thrive.

As outdoor space is at a premium, the owner quietly accommodated the front lawn to plant a few vegetables and creepers. 'Most people can't identify the vegetables from the creepers', says Varady.

PHOTOGRAPHY BY **Stephen Varady**

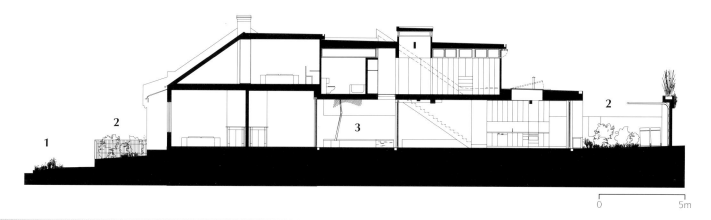

1 Nature strip
2 Garden
3 Courtyard

0   5m

INSIDER'S TIP

A clever placement of a courtyard can expand the sense of space from inside. It also provides the benefit of useable outdoor space, something that many of these cottages lack.

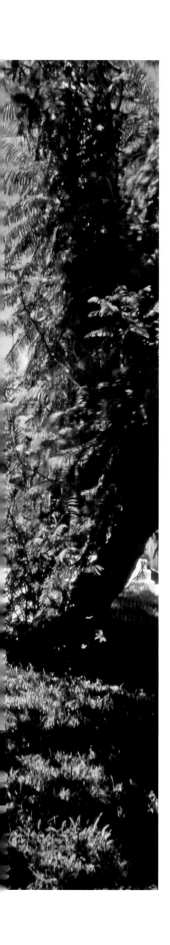

MOVING ON FROM
THE 1970s

There are few signs of the house from the front gate. Located on a battleaxe-shaped block, at the end of a no-through road, the only things that are visible are the trees. It's only when you walk along a side path that the house comes into view. 'It's quite an oasis', says Varady, who renovated the house as well as laying out the new garden beds and terrace.

Originally built in the late 19th century, the house had been altered in the 1970s. However, with that period returning to favour, the owners and architect decided to keep some of the features of that time. One area that needed to be addressed was a lack of connection to the garden. As a consequence, several internal walls were removed and new glazed doors were added.

ARCHITECT **Stephen Varady Architecture**

One of the main problems with the original garden was that it sloped towards the rear of the property. Varady designed two new levels for the garden, with the upper level comprising a lawn area, as well as a large terrace finished with concrete pavers. And to create a dramatic vista from the living room and front entrance, a raised pond was included in the design. So that the goldfish could be seen while sitting on the terrace, Varady included a toughened glass wall in the pond. 'You don't want to be continually standing up and looking in', says Varady, who worked closely with the owners in selecting plants.

In keeping with the 1970s spirit, vibrant colour appears on the darker side of the house with magenta and lime-green rendered walls. Inside, the walls are white. 'There's quite a contrast in the colour scheme between the indoors and outdoors. The owners wanted to be able to display their artwork against a neutral backdrop', says Varady.

PHOTOGRAPHY BY **Stephen Varady**

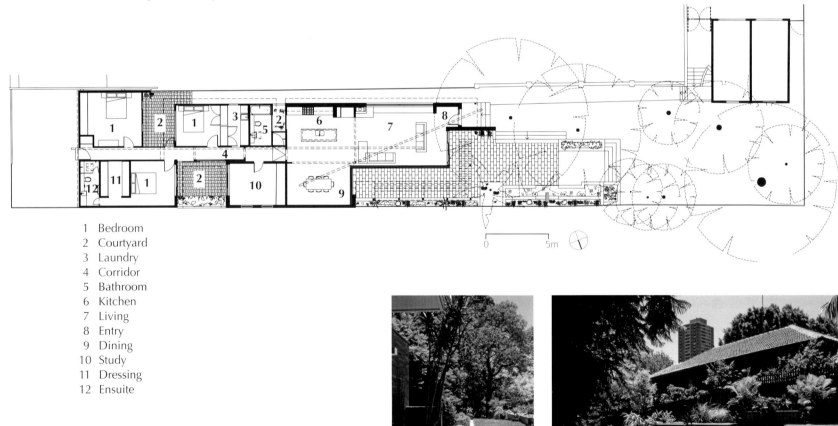

 1 Bedroom
 2 Courtyard
 3 Laundry
 4 Corridor
 5 Bathroom
 6 Kitchen
 7 Living
 8 Entry
 9 Dining
10 Study
11 Dressing
12 Ensuite

0   5m

INSIDER'S TIP

Be brave with colour. If it's used in the right place, it can have an impact.

SCULPTURAL FORMS

This house designed by Alex Popov is on a steep site, staggered over three levels. The lowest level, shared by adjoining properties, fronts the water. 'It can get fairly cold down here, with the westerly winds', says landscape architect Daniel Baffsky, principal of 360°.

As the house is perched on a cliff, entry to the home is via the top level, which includes the garage. While there is a garden at street level, the owners of this house gravitate to the courtyard garden on the middle level. Adjoining the dining and formal living areas, this courtyard provides a protective nook against the coastal elements.

Floor-to-ceiling glass bi-fold doors connect the living areas to the courtyard, with both areas featuring limestone floors. Like the interior, which is minimally furnished, the courtyard garden is also pared back. The main feature of the courtyard is a large wall sculpture by artist Janet Lawrence. Made from copper and glass, the sculpture forms an important backdrop for both the external and internal spaces.

Initially, the courtyard was going to be void of any plants. However, when the sculpture was placed in situ, it became clear that a plant equally as sculptural could form an interesting juxtaposition. A Japanese maple, with gnarled branches and asymmetric form was selected for the courtyard. 'In autumn, the changing colours of the leaves play beautifully with the copper', says Baffsky.

As sandstone lay beneath the terrace, it was decided to create a raised garden bed rather than excavate. The gentle mound is planted with baby's tears, native button fern and dampiera that covers the base of the mound. 'The dampiera has a small, delicate but vibrant purple flower. It's long flowering and quite magical', says Baffsky, who enclosed the garden bed with a 120-millimetre-high stainless steel edge. The thin edge provides minimal retaining and allows the baby's tears to spill over and blur the edge of the mound.

So as not to deflect from the sculpture, the maple has been planted slightly off-centre. 'It's unusual for a landscape to follow a sculpture and the tree is sculptural in itself, so it was important that they were complementary. The way the tree leans into the sculpture ... it's like they're talking to each other', says Baffsky.

PHOTOGRAPHY BY **Rodney Evans; Toby Burrows**

DESIGNED TO MOVE

This house, by Paul Uhlmann Architects, was designed to move. The house is located in an erosion precinct near a beach. 'A council condition was that the house had to be able to be moved with as little as 12 hours notice', says Uhlmann, conscious of the need to beat the rising water.

The water may not rise for years, so it still seemed appropriate to design a house and garden that would be enjoyed by a family with young adult children. In three segments, the house is raised above the ground for possible future towing. 'It's almost like a moveable piece of furniture. In the case of rising water, a trolley system is used to transport the house away, hence the three sections', says Uhlmann, who worked closely with landscape architect Sheryn Da-Re of Design Team Ink.

The steel-framed house is clad in plywood and features extensive glazing. Above each metal roof is sailcloth, creating additional protection against the elements. Linking the three pods are generous timber decks. One timber deck runs through the centre of the house between the living areas and main bedroom. There is also a larger deck that extends across the rear of the house, designed over two levels.

ARCHITECT
Paul Uhlmann Architects

LANDSCAPE ARCHITECT
Design Team Ink

With timber floors inside and timber decks surrounding the house, there's informality in the design. 'The steps to the garden are quite broad and deliberately open tread. The idea is to lose the sand through the gaps in the treads before entering the house', says Uhlmann, who included cane light fittings by New Zealand designer David Trubridge on both the ceiling of the deck and in the living areas. 'It's a fairly loose division between the indoor and outdoors', says Uhlmann.

The courtyard-style garden to the rear of the house is also fairly loose in structure. White sand intersects curved stone garden beds filled with rocks and pebbles. The band of sand and rock beds has a wave-like pattern and, depending on the amount of foot traffic, changes formation. Design Team Ink also used local species for the garden: tuckeroos, pandanus trees and casuarinas, endemic to the northern New South Wales coastline. Also included in the design are an outdoor shower, a plunge pool and built-in seating. 'The courtyard is an extension of the house. It's not precious. After all, it could disappear with short notice', says Uhlmann.

PHOTOGRAPHY BY **David Sandison**

INSIDER'S TIP

There's no point investing too much money in a garden if it's likely to experience a change in conditions.

GARDEN OF REFLECTIONS

Designed by Allen Jack + Cottier, this house overlooks Sydney Harbour from its cliff-side location. The interior circulation is relatively complex, encompassing several levels. The design intent was to treat the outdoor areas as additional rooms and thus well-respected landscape architect Vladimir Sitta of Terragram was commissioned for this project.

Water, in a number of guises, was initially intended to act as a guide and companion to visitors once they passed through the threshold between common and uncommon ground at street level. However, the budget didn't allow for the amount of water originally envisaged, so the sound of water invites visitors to proceed past the roof garden to the interior.

The roof garden is dissected by granite slabs that undulate and gradually increase in height to allow for the planting of small shrubs above the garage's concrete slab. A long flight of cantilevered and stainless steel-clad concrete stairs leads to the main entrance. An off-white limestone bridge links the outside to the inside. Wide steps leading towards the entrance continue under the house, as does the water surface.

ARCHITECT
Allen Jack + Cottier

LANDSCAPE ARCHITECT
Terragram

Terragram included a bamboo grove in the design. Horizontal, light-reflecting zigzagging slabs of laminated glass discharge water into a pool at the end of the property, filling the garden with the sound of running water. At night the effect of the glass is further enhanced by dozens of regularly inserted fibre-optic lights, creating an entrancing atmosphere.

A central double-height volume courtyard functions as a sculpture court and is entirely filled with water. 'This space reflects the sun and moon into the interior spaces. Here, the connection to Sydney Harbour becomes apparent', says Sitta. The swimming pool is located at the edge of the cliff face.

PHOTOGRAPHY BY **Vladimir Sitta and Rod Parry**

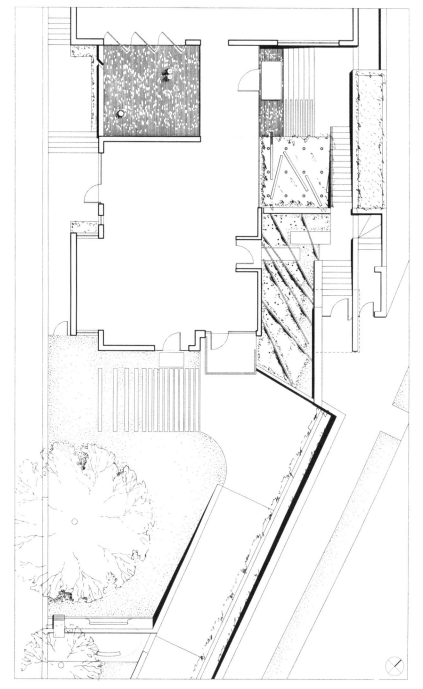

INSIDER'S TIP

It's important to create a
journey through the garden
as well as through the house.
There should be an element
of surprise, whether it's
indoors or outdoors.

POST-VICTORIAN

From the wide leafy street, this Victorian terrace appears completely intact. With its wrought-iron lacework, the terrace is consistent with other period homes in the heritage streetscape. However, past the front door, there are few hallmarks of the past.

One of the main problems with the original terrace was its lack of connection to the outdoors. Reworked for a couple with two young children, the brief to Stanic Harding was to create a light-filled contemporary home, connected to the garden.

Unlike the original home, which accessed the garden via steep and rickety stairs, a new terrace leads directly from the lounge. Paved in granite and featuring a built-in timber seat, it's a space regularly used by the family. A raised garden bed, planted with succulents creates a private nook for outdoor dining. The terrace also acts as a plinth for the garage and undercroft spaces below. Stanic Harding converted one of these spaces to a workshop, another to a studio and a third to a wine cellar. 'The owner loves to paint down here', says architect Andrew Stanic, one of the directors of the practice.

ARCHITECT   **Stanic Harding Pty Ltd**

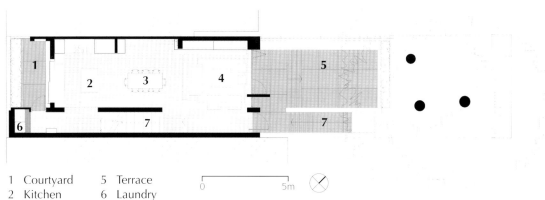

1 Courtyard   5 Terrace
2 Kitchen   6 Laundry
3 Dining   7 Stair
4 Living

0   5m

As the terrace is raised above the living areas, the garden can be appreciated from various aspects within the house. 'Views of the terrace can also be enjoyed from the bedrooms', says Stanic.

The kitchen, below street level, benefits from having a light court rather than a terrace. And although the view doesn't extend to leafy trees, there is a wonderful sandstone wall, covered with moss. While the kitchen could have been opened up to the front terrace with glass doors, the decision was made to create a large window instead. 'We didn't want to reduce the useable area in the kitchen. And when the window is opened, you feel connected to the courtyard', says Stanic.

PHOTOGRAPHY BY **Paul Gosney**

INSIDER'S TIP

If there are too many level changes between the indoor and outdoor spaces, the outdoors will be seen rather than used.

PRIVATE COURTYARDS

Designed by O'Connor + Houle Architecture, this house sits behind a large glass and steel screen. A gentle mound, sparsely planted with eucalypts, provides an alternative to the traditional front garden. 'The screen creates a sense of ambiguity. You're not quite sure where the building starts and where the garden ends', says architect Stephen O'Connor, who worked closely with his partner Annick Houle and landscape architect Elizabeth Peck.

Concealed behind the moody reflective glass screen is the first of several courtyards. The path to the front, which doubles as a courtyard, offers views into the house as well as through glass to the street. A second courtyard can be seen from the entrance. Located at the end of a gallery/corridor, this compact courtyard (1 by 5 metres) creates a vista from the front door, as well as an outlook for the second bedroom. Simply planted with Japanese maples and volcanic rocks, it also extends the sense of space within the home.

A larger courtyard, oriented to the north, provides the main outdoor space for the owners. Accessed from the kitchen and living areas via large sliding doors, as well as a large glass pivotal door, this courtyard is treated by O'Connor + Houle as an extension of the house. The external walls,

ARCHITECT
O'Connor + Houle Architecture

LANDSCAPE ARCHITECT
Elizabeth Peck Landscape Architect

for example, are aligned with the walls in the living areas and kitchen. The 2.4-metre wall in the courtyard was constructed in the same grey bricks. 'We saw the courtyard as part of the building and, like a room, privacy was important', says O'Connor.

The main courtyard is planted with a solitary eucalypt and features granite pavers. The other feature in the courtyard is a reflective pond, strategically positioned outside a low-level window to the main bedroom. Sunlight from the water is reflected onto the bedroom walls, creating a meditative environment.

Triple-glass-panelled doors framing the dining area can be pulled back to allow the courtyard to feel part of the interior spaces. With a barbeque and enough room for a table and chairs, the courtyard also functions as a more informal place to eat. 'It's a relatively large house, on a relatively compact site. But you're always connected to the garden wherever you are in the house', says O'Connor, who also included a small courtyard to the rear of the house for drying clothes.

PHOTOGRAPHY BY **Trevor Mein**

INSIDER'S TIP

Align external spaces with the internal spaces. When walls are aligned, the two areas feel as one.

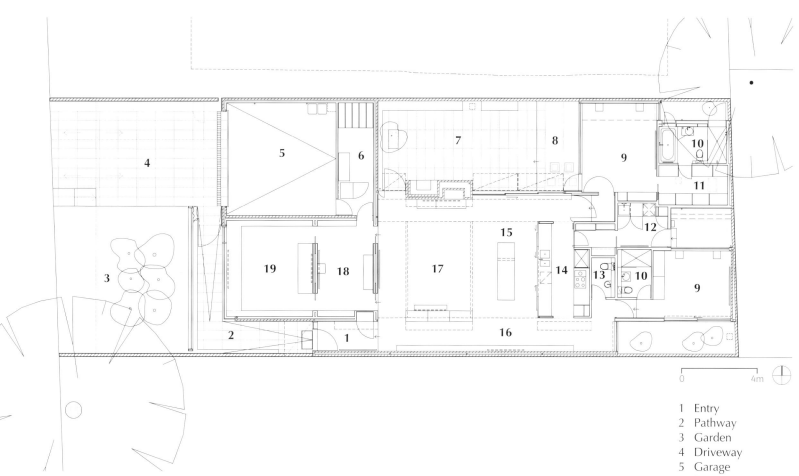

1 Entry
2 Pathway
3 Garden
4 Driveway
5 Garage
6 Store
7 Courtyard
8 Pool
9 Bedroom
10 Bathroom
11 WIR
12 Laundry
13 WC
14 Kitchen
15 Dining
16 Gallery
17 Living
18 Reading
19 Study

A CLUSTER OF BIRCH TREES

The front garden of this period house is typical of many in the leafy street. With an iron fence and neat front lawn, its main feature is an established Jacaranda tree. One of the brightest colours seen from the street is a vibrant orange-red front door. 'We wanted to indicate there was something less traditional behind the front door', says architect Stephen O'Connor, who worked closely with his partner, architect Annick Houle, renovating the house and designing the garden.

O'Connor + Houle Architecture created a new open-plan kitchen, living and dining area at the rear of the house, together with a separate study. Both areas look out to a low-maintenance garden. The main focus of the garden is a cluster of birch trees, planted on a narrow lawn area, adjacent to a 10-metre-long lap pool. 'We were advised not to plant the birch trees too closely together', says O'Connor, who preferred to place the trees only half a metre apart. 'We wanted the branches to become entangled. It gives them a sculptural quality', he adds.

The birch trees can be seen from the front door, creating an interesting vista for the owners as well as guests. The lap pool, placed to one side of the site, also provides an important aspect from the study. 'We aligned the pool to the study. The sight lines allow the owner to look down the entire length of the pool', says O'Connor, who used a pigmented concrete around the pool and terrace.

ARCHITECT
O'Connor + Houle Architecture

LANDSCAPE ARCHITECT
Elizabeth Peck Landscape Architect

O'Connor + Houle also included a plunge pool in the back garden. Unlike the lap pool, which is rendered in a grey quartz colour, the spa is lined with hot pink tiles. 'We're told by the owners that jumping into the pool is like jumping into a creek. They compare the spa to opening a bottle of champagne', says O'Connor, referring to the colour palette.

While the pool and spa occupy a significant part of the garden, there was sufficient space for an outdoor setting. O'Connor + Houle designed a concrete table that cantilevers over timber benches. Located adjacent to the informal living areas, this terrace is regularly used for alfresco dining.

Large glass doors (3.3 metres high) connect the living areas to the terrace. When the doors are left open, leaves occasionally blow into the house. 'Sweeping up a few leaves is as about as much work as it takes', says O'Connor, whose clients emphasised the need for a low-maintenance garden. 'They're both professionals. They didn't want to have to get the lawn mower out every second weekend. There is a small lawn, but that's more for a gentler surface and the colour', he adds.

PHOTOGRAPHY BY **Shannon Pawsey**

1	Front yard	9	Dining
2	Verandah	10	Garage
3	Bedroom	11	Lawn
4	Dressing	12	Pool
5	Bathroom	13	Study
6	Laundry	14	Kitchen
7	Courtyard	15	Hallway
8	Living	16	Lounge

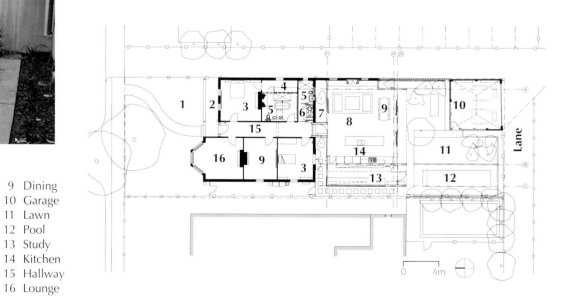

INSIDER'S TIP

A few highlight colours can enrich a garden, as well as adding an element of surprise.

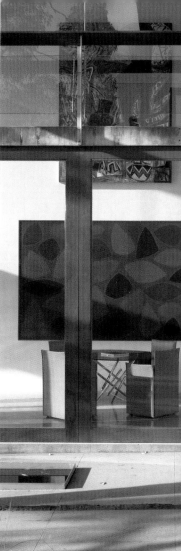

THE SAME MATERIALS

Landscape architect Phoebe Pape used the same materials as those used for the house when designing these outdoor spaces. The house, designed by Stutchbury + Pape, is quite raw with its off-formed concrete walls and floors. 'I wanted to use the same language in the garden', says Pape.

The house, on a steep site, edges towards the water. Designed over three levels, the entrance to the house is via the top level. 'We've used a series of retaining walls', says Pape, referring to the sandstone and concrete block walls leading to the front entrance. Mimicking the steel used for the internal staircase, a folded-steel staircase lightly cantilevers over these walls. 'We've used the most direct method of construction for the external stairs. They're clearly expressed in the landscape', says Pape.

Each of the retaining walls has been planted with eucalypts as well as low-maintenance plants. Native grasses in blues and greens soften each edge. The folded-steel steps lead to the top level of the house, which features a swimming pool. Designed with clear glass, light filters into the main terrace and courtyard, leading from the kitchen and living areas. Pape included a small patch of lawn, adjacent to the granite terrace, which offers views of established gum trees and water in the distance.

ARCHITECT **Stutchbury + Pape Architecture**

INSIDER'S TIP

Sometimes you need to overplant a garden to suppress weeds. It can still be low-maintenance.

There is a second courtyard at the lowest level. This courtyard links a detached studio to a study/second bedroom. Complete with a water feature made of steel, the courtyard also includes a barbeque and outdoor kitchen. And although it's open to the elements, there is some protection from the overhang to the floor above.

Originally, Stutchbury + Pape planned to have a shallow pond on the roof. This would have cooled the house down during the warmer months, as well as forming a link to the harbour beyond. However, neighbours were concerned that ducks would find a new home on the roof. 'We've used pebbles instead. It was a compromise that seems to please everyone', says Pape.

One of the main challenges of designing the landscape was removing the undergrowth that had developed over the years. 'There was a lot of lantana. It was one of the first things to be removed', says Pape. 'It's still quite a rustic garden, but it has been allowed to grow without all the undergrowth', she adds.

PHOTOGRAPHY BY **Michael Nicholson**

CONTACT DETAILS